Complementary Views of Western and Islamic Psychology of Religion

Religion and Psychology

Editor-in-Chief

Ralph W. Hood, Jr. (*University of Tennessee at Chattanooga, USA*)

Associate Editors

Mohammad Khodayarifard (*University of Tehran, Iran*)
Tomas Lindgren (*Umeå Universitet, Sweden*)
Tatjana Schnell (*Universität Innsbruck, Austria*)
Katarzyna Skrzypińska (*University of Gdańsk, Poland*)
W. Paul Williamson (*Henderson State University, Arkadelphia, USA*)

Volumes published in this Brill Research Perspective are listed at *brill.com/rpsys*

Complementary Views of Western and Islamic Psychology of Religion

By

Sevde Düzgüner

BRILL

LEIDEN | BOSTON

Library of Congress Control Number: 2022950652

Typeface for the Latin, Greek, and Cyrillic scripts: "Brill". See and download: brill.com/brill-typeface.

ISSN 2589-711X
ISBN 978-90-04-53502-2 (paperback)
ISBN 978-90-04-53503-9 (e-book)

Copyright 2023 by Sevde Düzgüner. Published by Koninklijke Brill NV, Leiden, The Netherlands.
Koninklijke Brill NV incorporates the imprints Brill, Brill Nijhoff, Brill Hotei, Brill Schöningh, Brill Fink, Brill mentis, Vandenhoeck & Ruprecht, Böhlau, V&R unipress and Wageningen Academic.
Koninklijke Brill NV reserves the right to protect this publication against unauthorized use. Requests for re-use and/or translations must be addressed to Koninklijke Brill NV via brill.com or copyright.com.

This book is printed on acid-free paper and produced in a sustainable manner.

Contents

Abstract   1

Keywords   1

1   A Short History of Western Psychology   1

   1.1   *Definitions of the Human*   2

   1.2   *The Common Roots of Psychology, Philosophy, and Religion*   3

   1.3   *The Establishment of Western Psychology*   5

   1.4   *Approaches to Religion in Western Psychology*   7

2   A Short History of Islamic Psychology   16

   2.1   *Descriptions of the Human in the Holy Quran*   17

   2.2   *Descriptions of the Human in the Hadiths of the Prophet Muhammad (PBUH)*   19

   2.3   *Descriptions of the Human by Muslim Scholars*   22

   2.4   *Academic and Institutional Backgrounds of Islamic Psychology*   25

3   How to Combine Western and Islamic Psychologies   29

   3.1   *The Contact between Western and Islamic Psychologies*   30

   3.2   *Islamic Psychology and Sufi Psychology*   37

   3.3   *Sensitive Points in Studying Islamic Psychology*   44

     3.3.1   Denial of Psychology   44

     3.3.2   Disregard of Religion/Islamic View in Psychology   44

     3.3.3   Superficial Approach   45

     3.3.4   Confusion of Concepts   45

     3.3.5   Translation Challenges   45

     3.3.6   Measurement Challenges   46

     3.3.7   Practice Challenges   46

   3.4   *The Combination of Western and Islamic Psychologies*   47

4   Complementary Views of Western and Islamic Psychologies   54

   4.1   *Complementary Views on the Islamic Model of the Human*   55

     4.1.1   Ruh   55

     4.1.2   Nafs   56

     4.1.3   Qalb   57

     4.1.4   'Aql   60

     4.1.5   Fitrah   61

     4.1.6   Interaction among Basic Concepts of Islamic Psychology   62

   4.2   *Complementary Views on the Psychospiritual Development of Human*   65

     4.2.1   *Nafs al-ammarah* (The Commanding Nafs)   65

4.2.2 *Nafs al-lawwamah* (The Accusing Nafs) 67

4.2.3 *Nafs al-mulhimah* (The Inspired Nafs) 71

4.2.4 *Nafs al-mutma'innah* (The Satisfied/Peaceful Nafs) 73

4.2.5 *Nafs ar-radhiyyah* (The Well-Pleased Nafs) 74

4.2.6 *Nafs al-mardhiyyah* (The Well-Pleasing Nafs) 76

4.2.7 *Nafs al-kamilah* (The Mature/Perfect Nafs) 77

4.3 *Complementary Views on Selected Stories from Rumi's* Mathnawi 79

4.3.1 The Story of Nay 79

4.3.2 The Sultan and the Handmaid 81

4.3.3 Allah (JJH) and the Prophet Moses (PBUH) 82

4.3.4 The Dragon Hunter 84

4.3.5 The Young Man and Thorns 85

4.4 *Complementary Views on Physical, Psychosocial, and Spiritual Health* 86

5 Conclusion 92

Acknowledgments 96

References 96

*This monograph is only and solely dedicated to
Prof. Ralph. W. Hood, a distinguished scholar who encouraged
and inspired me most in my whole life*

Know that the wheeling heavens are turned by waves of love:
Were it not for Love, the world would be frozen (inanimate).
How would an inorganic thing disappear (by change) into a plant?
How would vegetive things sacrifice themselves to become
(endowed with) spirit?
How would the spirit sacrifice itself for the sake of that
Breath by the waft whereof a Mary was made pregnant?
Each one (of them) would be (as) stiff and immovable as ice:
How should they be flying and seeking like locusts?
Every mote is in love with that Perfection and hastening upward
like a sapling.
Their haste is (saying implicitly) *"Glory to God (Allah)!"*

MAWLANA JALALUDDIN RUMI, *Mathnawi*, v. 5, c.3854–3859
(couplets translated by R.A. Nicholson)

Complementary Views of Western and Islamic Psychology of Religion

Sevde Düzgüner
Department of Psychology of Religion, Faculty of Theology,
Marmara University, Türkiye
sevde.duzguner@marmara.edu.tr

Abstract

Publications about Islam and psychology have increased in number over the past few decades. Empirical research and therapy practices for Muslims have attracted academic attention. However, the theoretical basis of studying in both Western and Islamic psychologies is not clear yet. Taking a step back, this monograph presents the emergence, first contact, and coexistence of the human theories of Western psychology and the human model of Islamic psychology in general and Sufi psychology in particular. Then it suggests a complementary approach method on how to utilize both by considering the background of each. The approach is discussed in detail with examples, from the stories of Rumi to psychotherapy practices.

Keywords

psychology of religion – religious psychology – Islamic psychology – Sufi psychology – psychospiritual development – health – *qalb* (heart) – *'aql* (reason) – *nafs* (psyche) – *ruh* (soul) – *Tasawwuf* (Sufism)

1 A Short History of Western Psychology

Psychology, which develops theory, research, and practice, aims to investigate the human being from various aspects. Psychology studies carried out to date have presented valuable information to understand human beings, but they have also raised new questions. While these questions are new to psychology, they are not new to humanity. Throughout history, humanity has been engaged in an effort to understand her/himself. Therefore, explanations that give different answers to the question of "who the human is" have emerged over time.[1]

1.1 Definitions of the Human

Since the earliest periods, the human has sought answers to several existential questions, such as who she/he is, where she/he comes from, and what the meaning of life is. On the one hand, many thinkers, clergymen, writers, scholars, and poets have produced various ideas about these issues. On the other hand, religions also present explanations about humans; in particular, holy scriptures include many descriptions of the features of her/him. So, the question "who the human is" is answered in two different sources. The first source is the answers given by Allah (JJH), God, or the transcendent being through holy scriptures, revelations, and religious sources in general. The second source is the human her/himself. Humans' efforts of self-understanding were previously included in philosophy, which is used for all thinking activities of humankind, including arts and literature. Then, positivistic sciences attempted to find explanations through a set of research and measurement methods. Psychology, which directly examines human beings, was founded as an independent discipline in the nineteenth century and developed theories about humans apart from the speculative method of philosophy and normative explanations of religions. Since the human is a multi-dimensional and very complicated being,

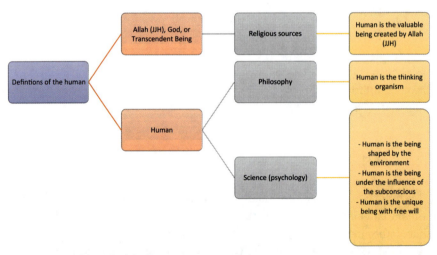

FIGURE 1   Definitions of the human
SOURCE: AYTEN AND DÜZGÜNER 2017: 16

---

[1] In fact, the appropriate question is what the human is, but we wanted to deal with the question of who, not what, since the human is an honorable being.

psychology has put forth different approaches to her/him over time. Figure 1 presents the definitions of the human as the sources, means, and examples.

There are three main roads to answer the question of what kind of being the human is: religion, philosophy, and scientific psychology. Although scientific psychology was established by a separation from religion and philosophy, psychology is deeply rooted in them. The relation between these three fields has been shaped by the historical changes in the perception of humans and higher beings. Psychology has developed due to the change in the view of the relation between body and soul/spirit. Likewise, the psychology of religion has developed due to the change in the view of the relation between the human and transcendent being(s).

1.2   *The Common Roots of Psychology, Philosophy, and Religion*

It is frequently stated that psychology exists wherever and whenever humans exist. Regardless of time and geography, people have physiological needs such as food, shelter, and physical health, as well as psychological needs such as trust, empathy, and guidance. Historical sources indicate that there were practitioners who met the physiological needs of people in the earliest periods, as well as practitioners who met their psychological needs as well. These practitioners have been called by names such as a magician, magician doctor, shaman, soothsayer, fortune teller, or wise man in different cultures and periods. The craft of these practitioners was a combination of medicine, religion, and psychology (Benjamin 2019: 1–2). In these practices, the belief in spirit/soul was quite decisive.

In ancient times, the belief in the existence of good and bad spirits and the belief that the soul leaves the body during the dream are examples of the common roots of psychology and religious belief. Physical and mental diseases were explained by the influence of these souls/spirits. Since there were no clear boundaries between medicine and psychology at that time, psychological and medical diseases were considered together (Hothersall 1984: 3). As a result of this, psychological issues were discussed in light of the opinions of physicians about the body and soul/spirit, which were shaped by religious belief. For instance, the belief that humans should be prepared for the next life led to increased research and knowledge about the soul and body in Egyptian civilization. This belief-based research helped in the accumulation of very rich knowledge of observation and practice that were the first seeds of scientific methodology. The belief in the idea of "the human who becomes union with nature" of Indian civilization is also important in terms of reflecting today's Far Eastern and Central Asian perspectives. Even today the Yin and Yang elements are at the center of the belief and thought system of Chinese culture. This holistic approach was associated with health and happiness in a psychological context. Likewise, the cause of all types of diseases in the Mesopotamian civilizations from the Sumerians to the Acadians is the sins committed intently or accidentally. The practitioner, who can be described as a physician-priest, interviews the patient to discover this sin and asks the patient to open her/his heart to him. A book from that period, *Patient Interview Guide for The Medicus*, presents some questions from these interviews: "Did you create trouble between father and son or mother and daughter, did you say yes where you should have said no, did you use wrong weights on the scales, did you steal, did you carry truth only on your lips and dishonesty in your heart" (Babaoğlu 2002: 21–31). So, it is clear that religious belief and physiological and psychological health are intertwined in ancient civilizations since belief determines the mentality of the period and its approach to the human.

It is known that there was a similar approach in the ancient Greek civilization, regarded as the root of modern psychology. For example, known as the "father of medicine/psychology," Hippocrates (d. 370 BC) rejected the idea that diseases are caused by supernatural powers. However, he was not opposed to religious belief. According to him, medicine was a divine art; God and the healing powers of nature help physicians to treat the patient (Kahya 1998: 120). Socrates (d. 400 BC) and Plato (347 BC) adopted the immortality of the soul and belief in God as creator (Erdem 1999: 158). Even Aristotle's (d. 322 BC) naturalistic, physiological, and empirical approach is limited to the issues of learning, memory, sleep, and dreams, routine perceptions, animal behaviors, emotion, and motivation. Rejecting the strict materialistic claim that the mind and the soul are the same he distinguishes these two by saying the mind is impassible intellectual apprehension and unlike the mind, the soul is imperishable (Robinson 1995: 48). Based on these, there is a relationship between body (substance) and soul/spirit (form). The soul (telos) is the purpose that activates the body and makes it alive. God is the pure form, the first mover, non-substance. His essence is thinking. God is the one. He is not a creator but the one who shapes and moves (Erdem 2000: 268). Seeing the soul as impossible to be observed, Aristotle is concerned with the question "how does it work," not "what is it" depending on the reason and behavior (Bruno 1996: 11).

As seen, every attempt to explain the human in antiquity also handled soul/spirit and God. The emergence of Christianity led to a new approach to the relationships between body and soul/spirit, and also the relationship between the human and God. Christian philosophy emerged over time and until the thirteenth century, the medieval view of human consciousness was viewed as sense, reason, and intellect under the light of the metaphor of the Holy Trinity (Robinson 1995: 102). The church gained power as a religious institution and the clergy became authorities in many areas – individual, social, economic, and political. In such an atmosphere, psychological disorders were left to the opinion of the church for centuries. The human soul/spirit was seen as an extension of the Holy Spirit. Therefore, it was accepted that the soul/spirit never becomes ill, but it can be captured by the devil; so, the clergy created exorcist rituals (Babaoğlu 2002: 61–62). Since the philosophers and writers of the Middle Ages were sure that the philosophical ideas in the Bible were the best way to knowledge, their ideas about the human, namely Christian psychology studies, were the result of personal ideas dependent on religion instead of research and observation (Johnson and Jones 2000: 16). Christian thought on body and soul was influential for centuries.

In sum, it can be stated that the philosophical foundations of psychology are intertwined with beliefs about unseen beings/deities such as the soul/spirit and God because belief (which is the basis of religion in history), thought (which is the basis of philosophy), and human perception (which is the basis of psychology) intertwined and influenced each other.

1.3 The Establishment of Western Psychology

Western psychology depends on the emergence of a positivistic scientific approach that dates back to the thirteenth century in Europe. In that period, there had been a leap in many fields, such as science, philosophy, art, and literature. Thus, the first traces of the conceptual framework of modern science began to emerge; for example, research centers such as universities and hospitals were established at this time. However, a completely positivistic scientific approach had not yet emerged since the authoritarian church tried to keep these institutions under its domination. The church supported the establishment of universities and hospitals to manage them for its own purposes (Güngörmüş-Kona 2005: 29–30).

The geographical discoveries that began in the fifteenth century, new developments in technology, the emergence of the bourgeoisie class, and financial development weakened the authority of the church. With the Renaissance and the Reformation, rationality came to the fore, which is the basis of a positivistic scientific approach. Copernicus's (d. 1543) solar-centric system theory and Galileo's (d. 1642) invention of the telescope led to a change in the perception of the human. The view that the earth is an ordinary planet in the solar system and that the human is an ordinary being belonging to the class of living organisms led to the idea that both earth and human can be examined and explained within a new approach (Crapps 1986: 3–4). This approach was clarified over time with the ideas of philosophers. Descartes's "reflex movements" (undulatis reflexa) can be seen as a precursor to the ideas advanced by behavioral psychologists. His ideas led the attention of thinkers to mental processes rather than a mythological perception of soul/spirit. Descartes's idea that the brain is the most important organ in the emergence of behavior also contributed to this orientation (Fancher 1997: 42–43). Although these views were the philosophical basis of psychology, Descartes also included religion in his views. He tries to prove the existence of God by starting from the proposition "I think, therefore I am." Since the concept of God in the consciousness does not come from the obtained information via senses, it is an innate concept in the human soul/spirit (Erdem 1999: 63–64). Moreover, he claimed that he proved the existence of God in *Discours de la Méthode* (*Discourse on the Method*) (Adam 1963: 41).

Likewise, Locke's (d. 1704) *tabula rasa* played an important role in the emergence of scientific psychology. Although Locke did not admit that the idea of God is innate, he claimed that the idea of God can be reached. To him, God exists, and He determines the divine and moral rules (Çetin 1994: 171). While accepting the existence of divine rules, Locke (1992) underlined his empiricist approach by arguing that these rules are not the source of knowledge. Thus, it was one step closer to making an explanation about human beings without referring to religion. Locke's ideas were developed in various ways by thinkers who followed. His view that matter consists of the qualities ascribed to it and the idea of matter is not experimental is a fundamental element in Berkeley's (d. 1753) thought system. Locke's other view that there is no soul apart from the qualities attributed to it and it cannot be revealed by experiment was taken up and elaborated by Hume (d. 1776). Berkeley's idea that to exist is to be perceived helped the mind and perception issues to come to the fore (Bruno 1996: 47–48; Schultz and Schultz 2002: 77). It was Hume who clearly rejected the ontological existence of soul/spirit and drew attention to inner experiences. Emphasizing perceptions, imaginations, memories, and emotions, he focused on the mental functions and emotional experiences (Gökberk 1993: 347). Then, Leibnitz (d. 1716) developed the monadology theory and claimed that the physical world and mental experiences are two different aspects of the same reality. The mind consisted of monads as the body was made up of atoms, and monads played an important role in mental processes (Bruno 1996: 59–60; Schultz and Schultz 2002: 500). On the other hand, Kant (d. 1804) put forth that experiences cannot be explained solely by events that take place outside of humans. Rather, the person ultimately constructs her/his experiences (Benjafield 1996: 37). Thus, the importance of mental processes was underlined rather than the soul/spirit itself. Then, how the mind works came to the fore. Also, passive consciousness left its place to the active mind. These developments were an indication that psychology was on the way to becoming a science.

With the influence of the French Revolution (1789), many philosophical, social, political, and religious changes took place in the eighteenth century. The widespread acceptance of the superiority of reason shaped philosophical thinking and scientific developments. An emphasis on scientific knowledge based on evidence was the basis of the developments in the following century (Güngörmüş-Kona 2005: 74). In terms of psychology, mental processes, sensations, and perceptions were on the agenda of the thinkers and the experimental approach began to be adopted. Darwin's (d. 1882) theories of natural selection and evolution were effective on the human becoming a subject for scientific research. This theory was considered important in terms of pointing out the biological origins of humans and showing that the organism adapts to the environment. Also, this was an explanation of the human and the universe without any reference to the idea of God or soul/spirit.

By the end of the nineteenth century, the subjects of psychology started to be handled experimentally and statistically with the influence of Galton (d. 1911), Herbart (d. 1841), Weber (d. 1920), Fechner (d. 1887), and Helmholtz (d. 1894). In that period there was a common sense about the necessity of psychology to be an independent scientific discipline, and Wundt (d. 1920) explicitly expressed this opinion in the preface of his book *Grundzüge der Physiologischen Psychologie* (*Principles of Physiological Psychology*) published in 1874. He founded psychology as an independent discipline with the psychology laboratory at the University of Leipzig in 1879. He started to publish the journal *Philosophistiche Studien* (*Philosophical Studies*), the publication of this laboratory in 1881, changing the name of the journal to *Psychologie Studien* (*Psychology Studies*) in 1906. Thus, psychology was established and began to publish scientifically. Even though Wundt saw psychology as a separate branch of science, he was criticized for not regarding it as a natural science. Indeed, the scientific identity of psychology was clarified by the fact that psychologists who followed Wundt attached importance to measurable and empirical studies. However, the scope and methods of psychology have changed and varied over time based on different approaches to the human. Qualitative and phenomenological approaches gained importance later, especially with studies on cultural and religious effects on humans.

1.4   *Approaches to Religion in Western Psychology*

In general, the sources of the history of science underline that science reaches information with a method separate from normative religious and speculative philosophical explanations. These sources argue that with the establishment of scientific psychology, human beings began to be explained by scientific methods without referring to philosophical and religious sources. Many scholars claim the Renaissance was a movement away from the church, but *this is not the case*. In particular, the humanism of the Renaissance is inconceivable without religion, namely Christianity (Robinson 1995: 120). In addition to scientific methods, psychologists were frequently utilized from religious, philosophical, and mythological sources. The undeniable effect of belief on people has been decisive on this.

The belief in a supreme power is as old as the human effort to understand herself/himself. Throughout history, people have believed in many beings and meanings that they consider sacred and they have determined their lives within the framework of these beliefs. Although their names, contents, and practices have changed, religious or mystical beliefs have existed in all periods and cultures. These beliefs have the power to influence, change, transform, and rebuild the individual and the society. Therefore, the emotions, thoughts, and behaviors of the human are shaped by the effect of her/his religious belief. The close relationship between religion and culture also draws attention to the social dimension of religious faith. Psychologists, who are aware of the psychological and social effects of religious belief, have also seen religion as a subject of psychological research. Although approaches to religion in the field of psychology differ in favor of or against religion, it can be said that psychology and religion have always been in relation. Becoming stronger today, the relationship between religion and psychology is described by Köse as "sisters/brothers in an on-again-off-again relationship" (2006: 11). So, Western psychology is not reckless to religion even though some psychologists are. The background of the psychology of religion explains the case well. An overview of the development of the psychology of religion shows how religion and psychology interrelated and how the Christian perspective was influential, which is summarized below (see Düzgüner 2017).

Psychology of religion covers the psychological investigation of belief, unbelief, and disbelief. The emergence of the psychology of religion is almost simultaneous with the establishment of psychology as a science. Most of the pioneers of psychology, such as James (d. 1910), Watson (d. 1958), Skinner (d. 1990), Freud (d. 1939), Jung (d. 1961), Fromm (d. 1980), and Maslow (d. 1970), were interested in religion and put forward their theories and research, beginning with Wundt. Wundt devoted three volumes of his ten-volume comprehensive work *Völkerpsychologie* to his views on religion, naming this section "Myth and Religion." According to him, religion is the feeling that our world is a part of a larger, supernatural being, in which the goals that human beings most want to achieve are realized (Wulff 1997: 31). Wundt thought that the psychology of religion was also part of folk psychology, insisting on a historical, cultural, and anthropological basis. Therefore, he tried to deal with this field with a different method, which he called the "historical-comparative method." There is an obvious difference in understanding of religion between Wundt and American psychologists of religion. Wundt argued that the survey method was at an individual level and claimed that it was not suitable for the psychological research of religion (Belzen 2005: 817–820). While insisting on empirical research on personal psychological issues, Wundt claimed that the significant events and phenomena in human history go beyond personal investigation and experimental methods. For sure, this approach was not explicable in the language of natural science (Robinson 1995: 280). While Wundt discussed the phenomenon of religion as a subject of folk psychology, American and English psychologists of religion investigated the same subject as a problem of individual psychology, as had James.

Varieties of Religious Experience, published by James in 1902, is considered the foundation of this field of psychology of religion because it regards religion as a psychological experience and discusses topics such as prayer, mysticism, conversion, religion, and mental health, which are considered as the basic subjects of the psychology of religion today. What distinguishes James from other thinkers is that he focuses on individual religious experience rather than organized religious institutions. According to him, religion is "the emotions, actions, and experiences of human individuals insofar as they see themselves related to whatever they regard as divine." (1961: 50). Moreover, he emphasized that he did not go to church to worship and did not believe the Bible to be the holy word of God (Erdem 2013: 132). He pushed the institutional dimension of religion out of the field of interest and emphasized individual experience. Although James makes psychological explanations with an emphasis on religious experience, it can be said that his interpretive method is not very separate from philosophy. It has been argued that there are two basic traditions in the psychology of religion: the interpretive method and the statistical-empirical method. If James is considered the pioneer of the interpretive approach, Hall is the pioneer of the empiricist tradition (Hood and Spilka 2012: 130).

James's first doctoral student, Hall (d. 1924) contributed to the field with different methods. Being also one of the first students trained in Wundt's lab, Hall adopted both interpretive and empirical-statistical methods. Hall studied psychology at Harvard University and established the first psychology laboratory in the United States at Johns Hopkins University in 1883. He started publishing America's first psychology journal four years later. Moreover, he gave great support to the establishment of the American Psychology Association (APA) in 1892, which still maintains its authority in the field of psychology, later being elected its chair (Weiten 2001: 3). Being curious about religious development and expression, Hall researched children and adolescents based on Galton's survey method, thereby taking the first step in the use of statistical analysis in the psychology of religion. However, his studies on religious issues were not limited to the empirical-statistical method and/or positivistic scientific approach.

In his two-volume book *Jesus Christ in the Light of Psychology*, he interpreted the life of the Prophet Jesus (PBUH) using basic psychological concepts. He also claimed that psychological interpretations of textual and historical studies were the biggest hope for Christianity. As a practical believer, he asserted that these studies are necessary for a better religious faith (Ames 1919). This book is a good example of religion-based psychology. Hall also founded the *American Journal of Religious Psychology and Education* in 1904, changing its name to the *Journal of Religious Psychology* in 1912. Hall was the first president of the Clark School of Religious Psychology at the University of Clark, as well as the APA (Hood and Spilka 2012: 133–134).

Here can be seen the difference between the psychology of religion and religious psychology. Hall is known as one of the pioneers of scientific psychology because of his empirical studies. Yet, it is he who also made studies based on Christian teaching and who used the expression of "religious psychology." Although Hall adopted a religious psychology approach, his students had not adopted this phrase. For example, Starbuck (d. 1947), a student of both James and Hall, published his first book with the title *Psychology of Religion* in 1899 and popularized the phrase "psychology of religion." His survey published in 1912 on 1200 Protestants in late adolescence is a remarkable study as well (Hood and Spilka 2012: 134). Here we need to consider how the roots of both psychology of religion and religious psychology are Christianity-based in the West, which is a natural result of the reality that the perception of the term "religion" brings to mind the dominant belief in that culture. Hence, we can term these the psychology of Christianity and Christian psychology. However, psychology of religion continued to widen, with different attitudes toward religion as well. For instance, Leuba (d. 1946), who trained in Hall's Clark School, studied conversion via interviews. Unlike Hall, Leuba lost his faith in religion and claimed in his book *Psychological Origin and the Nature of Religion* that religion is a product of the human mind (Hood and Spilka 2012: 134). Thus, the scope of the psychology of religion expanded with different perspectives of scholars such as Hall who believes in religion, Leuba who does not have a religious belief, and James who focuses on personal religious experience rather than religious institutions. It can be said that psychology was arm-in-arm with philosophy and religion (mainly Christianity) after it became an independent discipline in the West. Over time, several approaches to religion emerged in the psychology literature depending on the school of thought, such as behaviorism, psychoanalysis, and humanism.

Behaviorist and psychoanalytic approaches began to be effective in the field of psychology around the 1930s, and the ideas of these schools about religion have influenced the field of psychology of religion. According to the behaviorist

VIEWS OF WESTERN AND ISLAMIC PSYCHOLOGY OF RELIGION

school, psychology should only investigate visible behavior. Watson, a professor of psychology at the laboratory at Johns Hopkins University founded under the leadership of Hall, argued that psychology should be a behavioral science in his article "Psychology as the Behaviorist Views It" for the first time. Watson's focus was that psychology should produce measurable, repeatable, and objective scientific knowledge as a natural science (1963: 2–3). Skinner, a famous behaviorist with his experiments on mice, rabbits, and pigeons (Weiten 2001: 9), argued that the human is also subject to conditioning processes like animals, and behavior is determined entirely by the environment under the influence of reward-punishment through reinforcers. This approach has given little place to religion-related issues in its publications and maintained the behavioral perspective about religious phenomena. According to Watson, religion is a tool to control the people developed by religious people in positions to influence others. The religious behavior system is gradually instilled into the individual through fear and the continuity of this behavior is ensured with an authoritarian attitude. Religion is doubly against science since it consolidates unverifiable dogmas such as believing in the existence of a soul separate from the body, and as it uses methods such as fear and authority that are considered negative in objective scientific research (Wullf 1997: 118). Likewise, Skinner (1972: 63) considered religion as a control mechanism and argued that belief in an all-seeing God ensures continuing religious behavior by making it impossible to escape from the punisher. Heaven and hell are nothing more than a reward and punishment. So, religious beliefs and religious behaviors consist of conditioning processes under the influence of environmental reinforcements. After Leuba, this is another clear distinction between psychology and religion as well as philosophy.

The second effective school in psychology is the psychoanalytic approach. Focusing on case analysis rather than experimental studies, Freud claimed that human behavior emerged under the effect of subconscious processes that she/he could not be aware of. Freud started to publish his ideas at a time when psychology was seeking its place in science, and as such he was criticized as being unscientific. However, his ideas found room in medical psychology (the former version of psychiatry) rather than physiological psychology (the former version of general psychology) (Robinson 1995: 323). To Freud, traumatic experiences of the individual in her/his infancy take a place in her/his subconscious affecting their whole life. He also claimed that personality consists of id, ego, and superego, and basic instincts are sexuality and aggression (Freud 2004: 83). Freud was the figure who included religion-related issues in his studies most. First, in his article "Obsessive Actions and Religious Practices" (2006c) he claimed that religious belief is an illusion and religious behavior is a kind of obsession. Then he asserted that belief in an all-powerful God is the desperation of primitive beliefs against nature, and the anger toward the father during infancy turned into guilt and glorification, which in *Totem and Taboo* (2006a) he termed the Oedipal complex. He also asserted that religion stems from the weakness and helplessness of the human against nature in the *Future of an Illusion* (2006b). In *Moses and Monotheism* (1998), God is an exalted father and Moses is the resurgence of suppressed emotions. There is the transformation of individual psychoanalysis into social psychoanalysis. In this book, Freud also utilized mythical, historical, anthropological, and philosophical sources extensively.

As a result of the emergence of behaviorism and psychoanalysis, interest in religion-related subjects declined in the field of psychology between 1930 and 1950 (Hood and Spilka 2012: 136). The behaviorist school excludes religion from the field of research, as it regards religion as an unobservable phenomenon that is a kind of human-made control mechanism. On the other hand, Freud claimed that since religion originates from helplessness and weakness it will disappear with the development of science. An ever-disappearing phenomenon is not a scientifically remarkable subject (Loewenthal 2017: 9). Even today, many psychologists and psychology departments, including those in Muslim countries, disregard religious belief and experience in their psychological studies.

It should be noted here that even if the number of religion-related studies in the literature decreased until the late 1950s, almost all leading psychologists discussed religion. Therefore, religion and psychology have always been in contact, but the strength of this relationship has changed occasionally. On the other hand, theologians started to be interested in psychology in those years as well. The concept of pastoral psychology developed during this period. Pastoral counseling, defined by the American Association of Pastoral Counselors (AAPC) as "exploration, clarification, and guidance of human life, both individual and corporate, at the experiential and behavioral levels through a theological perspective" (Hunsinger 1995: 1), is generally practiced as the support given by pastors. In the 1950s, religious education institutions such as Harvard Divinity School, Union Theological Seminary in Richmond, Union Theological Seminary in New York, and the Department of Religion at the University of Southern California included pastoral psychology in their curriculum (Emerson 2000: 252).

Additionally, the view that religion is not the subject of scientific research led to its anti-thesis, and the Society of the Scientific Study of Religion was established in 1949. The association launched the *Journal for the Scientific*

Study of Religion two years later. The Religious Research Association was established in 1951 and sponsored the establishing of the journal *Review of Religious Research* in 1959 (Hood and Spilka 2012: 137). These journals are still among the significant publishing on the psychology of religion. So, there was a mutual interest toward the other between psychology and religion/theology. Also, the psychology of religion and religious psychology approaches coexisted.

In the 1960s, the humanist approach opened a new door to research areas in psychology. Humanistic psychologists argued that human beings are neither the product of the environment, as behaviorists claim, nor the prisoner of suppressed traumas in childhood, as psychoanalysts claim. Humanists insisted on free will, potential development, and positive aspects of human beings. Maslow (2001: 8–9), the pioneer of the humanist school, argued that the human is a precious/unique being who has been born with a pure inner nature and a potential to develop her/himself. Insisting on people having an intrinsic orientation for self-development, Maslow stated that religions can contribute to this (2001: 111–112). Other humanist psychologists also asserted that religious belief can improve human beings, add meaning to their lives, and give them strength during troubles in life. As a result of the spread of these opinions and the supporting research, scientific interest in the psychology of religion increased and the scope of the psychology of religion expanded with additional subjects such as religious development, the meaning of life, and religious coping.

An important development that emerged in the second half of the twentieth century was that the APA announced a separate division for religion-related issues. This division had an interesting historical background. Following the rise of a Catholic atmosphere prevailing at the general assembly of the APA, members of the association were seriously against the behaviorist arguments, and at the general meeting in 1946 it was decided to establish the American Catholic Psychological Association (ACPA) as a separate institution in contact with the APA. This association had two main objectives: "(1) To bring psychology to Catholics, (2) To bring a Catholic viewpoint to psychology." Then, the association encouraged Catholic schools to offer psychology classes and Catholics to gain PhDs in psychology. However, in 1970, not only Catholics but also members with different views to religion took a place among the members of the association, and it was decided to change the name of the association to Psychologists Interested in Religious Issues (PIRI). With this revision, the bylaw was changed: "(1) to provide a forum for identification, study and interpretation of psychological issues of significance to religious groups; (2) to develop resources and services pertinent to the psychological problems of church groups; (3) to cooperate with other groups in advancing the application of psychology to religious issue" (Reuder 1999: 95). PIRI was included as the 36th Division of the American Psychological Association in 1976, and in 1993 the name of the division was officially determined as the Society for the Psychology of Religion (Reuder 1999). This historical background of the association provides a good example of the zeitgeist in the transition from religious psychology to psychology of religion and the Christianity-centered perception of the term religion.

Division 36 has experienced a similar process recently. While the majority of the members were Catholic a religious psychology approach was adopted. When the members consisted not only of Catholics but also other attitudes toward religion the name of the association was changed, and a psychology of religion approach was adopted. Then, in 2003 some members suggested changing the name of the association to the Society for the Psychology of Religion and Spirituality, claiming religion and spirituality are different phenomena; the amendment was rejected the following year. However, in 2011 the name change was accepted with a high vote of 82 percent, because most of the members of the association adopted the difference between religion and spirituality. This division is one of the leading institutions of psychology of religion, with its two journals, scientific congresses, and many studies today. Even the changes in the history of this division are sufficient to show the dynamic and expanding structure of the field of psychology of religion and the existence of religion-based psychology studies.

In sum, Western psychology has a long history that depends on different approaches to the human and God/transcendent being. It can be said that attention has shifted over time from the ontological existence of the soul/spirit to the psychological reality of perception, mind, and consciousness, and from the ontological existence of God to the idea of God, transcendent being, higher being, and the like. The axis shift in the body and soul/spirit interaction has led to modern psychology and the axis shift in perception of God/transcendent being has shaped the psychology of religion. Although the transitions between the centuries cannot be drawn with strict boundaries, the Western psychological approaches to body – soul/spirit and human – God/transcendent being in Western history are shown in Table 1.

Throughout history, the human character was handled mainly under two headings: nature and spirit. Those who focus on the former lean on naturalism, materialism, scientific determinism, and positivism, while those who focus on the latter lean on spiritualism, idealism, transcendentalism, and psychological indeterminism. There was a tendency to separate nature and the spirit from each other in the seventeenth century. However, the main event that leads to the emergence of science and psychology was not the separation the

TABLE 1 Historical flow of Western psychological approach to the relationships between body and soul/spirit as well as human and god/transcendent being

Historical period	Body–soul/ spirit	Human–god/ transcendent being
BC era and ancient civilizations	Soul/spirit = The invisible being that activates the body	Supernatural power dominating the world
AD era– 17th century	The separation of soul/spirit and self/psyche/*nafs* Reason as a function of soul/spirit	God referred by mono- theistic religions
17th century– 18th century	Mind and mental processes instead of soul/spirit	The idea of God instead of the existence of God
19th century– 20th century	Transition from passive mind to active consciousness Sub-consciousness/unconsciousness/ beyond consciousness	Religious belief being subject to psychological research
21st century	Soul-spirit/spirituality = The power that activates body, meaning, unification with the universe, connectedness etc.	God marked by monotheistic religions is different from transcendent being

SOURCE: DÜZGÜNER 2013A: 281

nature from the spirit but the change of the metaphor from nature to machine (Robinson 1995: 128, 143, 234). The natural and mechanical approach to human remained influential until the twentieth century. Interestingly today, in the twenty-first century, there is a shift in interest from the material to the spiritual or the transcendent in Western psychology again. Behind this transformation are the sociocultural causes and the change of the dominant paradigms, as in the previous centuries. Based on the idea that religion and spirituality are separated from each other, recent tendency invites the concept of spirit (soul) back into psychology in a new context. Insisting on experience instead of the ontological existence of spirit, spirituality also resembles the ideas of James. Experience-based spirituality accompanies a belief in higher invisible but felt phenomena. This new tendency is also a continuation of the long process examined above. It seems that this spirituality will lead more interaction among psychology, philosophy, and religion/beliefs, which never strictly separated from each other at all.

In conclusion, Western religious psychology, psychology of religion, and ultimately spiritual psychology have not actually developed linearly. Although the ratio varies, it is possible to see the studies of these three in every period. So, psychology and religion have always been related. Besides, Western scientific psychology and psychology of religion have spread to other countries over time. Even assuming that the human investigated by psychology is the same everywhere, it is clear that the religion investigated by the psychology of religion is not the same. For the rest of the world, the psychology of religion is an imported field anyway. Western psychology is an explanation of the human being, and Western psychology of religion is an explanation of the relationship between the human and transcendent being(s). While other countries import these two areas, explanations about the human and transcendent being in their own cultures continued to exist. Islamic countries have also hosted both Western understanding and the understanding of their own religion and culture that will lead to Islamic psychology.

2   A Short History of Islamic Psychology

With the foundation of Islam in the seventh century, a new civilization originating from the East emerged in history. Islam, which spread over a wide geographical area, enabled many different cultures and nations to come together under the same belief. As it can be understood from the fact that the first command of the Holy Quran is "read" (96/1)[2] knowledge, learning, thinking, and science have found the ground for rapid development in the Islamic regions. Therefore, Muslim scholars have undertaken important studies in many fields, such as the natural sciences, philosophy, medicine, and mathematics.

Muslim scholars have written on human psychology from the earliest times and named these studies as *'ilm un-nafs* (the science of self/psyche-psychology).[3] The term *nafs* (self/psyche) in Islamic literature means the psychological and spiritual existence of an individual (Haque 2004: 357–358). Today, *'ilm un-nafs*

---

2   The citations of the verses and the hadiths belong to the original Arabic texts that are the same all over the world. The translations in this monograph have been selected by the author by comparing various Turkish and English sources with the original texts and expressed in a plain language. These are based on the translation of the Holy Quran by Ahmed Ali and the book *Islam Through Hadiths* by the Presidency of Religious Affairs in Türkiye. Translations other than verses and hadiths are the author's, unless otherwise stated.

3   The languages of Islamic countries vary as well as their alphabets. Although the Latin and Arabic alphabets are used in general, there are also differences in these. Therefore, there are differences in the spelling of a Turkish, Arabic, or Persian word in its own language as well as in the English version. This monograph is based on the language and spelling of the original source.

mainly includes the subjects of psychology and philosophy. Also, some understandings endemic in geography or culture are added to this category. The Holy Quran and the Sunnah of the Prophet Muhammad (PBUH) have been the basis of *'ilm un-nafs* (Hökelekli 2005: 410).

2.1 Descriptions of the Human in the Holy Quran

According to Islam, God is the only one, Allah (JJH). He created the universe and humankind. The Prophet Adam (PBUH) is the first human on this earth. A prophet is a person chosen by Allah (JJH) to deliver His messages to the people. Once the people had been deprived over time of the belief in one God, Allah sent them prophets as a reminder. The Prophet Adam (PBUH) was the first and the Prophet Muhammad (PBUH) the last prophet. Between these two, Allah (JJH) revealed to many prophets, such as David (PBUH), Abraham (PBUH), Jacob (PBUH), Moses (PBUH), and Jesus (PBUH). The common message of all of them is that God is the only one.

Allah (JJH) sent holy books to some prophets. Those who were chosen as prophets are *nabi*, and those to whom a book was sent are *rasul*. Since Allah (JJH) sent four holy books there are four *rasul*s as well. Allah (JJH) sent the Holy Psalms to the Prophet David (PBUH), the Holy Torah to the Prophet Moses (PBUH), the Holy Bible to the Prophet Jesus (PBUH), and the Holy Quran to the Prophet Muhammad (PBUH). Revealed gradually over twenty-three years, the verses (*ayah*s) of the Holy Quran were recorded and preserved both by memorizing and writing. After the death of the Prophet Muhammad (PBUH), Abu Bakr, the leader of the Muslim community, gathered the Holy Quran as a manuscript and arranged it as they had memorized. The Holy Quran was copied by hand and delivered to Muslim communities in various regions in the time of the next leader, Omar. Over the following periods, the tradition of the preservation of the Holy Quran by both memorizing and writing continued. Those who know the whole Holy Quran in Arabic by heart are called *hafid*, and today countless *hafid*s are trained in many Muslim countries. With the invention of the printing press, the printing and distribution of copies of the Holy Quran increased, and with the development of digital technology, it was transferred to virtual platforms. Thus, this one-volume Holy Book survived to the present as the main source of Islam. According to the Holy Quran, Islam is the name of the comprehensive religion that began with the Prophet Adam (PBUH) and was completed with the Prophet Muhammad (PBUH).

Allah (JJH) gives explanations about humans in many verses of the Holy Quran. These verses give an Islamic answer to the question of "who a human is" that we mentioned above. Quranic understanding of human can be summarized with the following headings.

1. The existence of human is a whole, including before this World, World life, and after this World

Each individual has a unique personal existence. Before the creation of this world, Allah (JJH) created the *ruh*s (souls/spirits) of all humans and talked to them as the verse explains: *And recall (O Prophet) when your Lord brought forth descendants from the loins of the sons of Adam and made them witnesses against their own selves. asking them: "Am I not your Lord?" They said: "Yes, we do testify." We did so lest you claim on the Day of Resurrection: "We were unaware of this"* (7/172). So, the spiritual existence of the human being precedes this world. First, the ruhs of all people were created, then these ruhs came to this world. They are born as babies after reaching a body and become alive. As explained in the following verse, the life of this world is a place of test for human: *Verily We created the human from a drop of mingled sperm, in order to test him: So, We gave him (the gifts), of Hearing and Sight* (76/2).

The human who completes her/his life in this world dies. In other words, the *ruh* leaves the body in due course and migrates to the hereafter. There, a new life begins depending on her/his deeds in the world: *Say: Allah (JJH) brings you to life, then He makes you die. Then gathers you on the Day of Resurrection about which there is no doubt* (45/26). Islam considers the human being as a whole and unique being.

2. The human is the most honorable and supreme being

The human is created by Allah (JJH) as honorable being and superior to many beings. Everything in this world gains meaning with the existence of the human. Allah (JJH) called the human *my caliph [trustee] on earth* (2/30). What makes the human valuable in the sight of Allah (JJH) is that she/he is a rational being and has free will. Unlike other living things, the human does not act based only on instincts and she/he chooses her/his own actions by thinking and decision-making.

Allah (JJH) states that He has put the earth at the service of humanity: *Indeed We have honored the children of Adam, and carried them over land and sea, provided them with good things for their sustenance, and exalted them over many of Our creatures* (17/70). But He has conferred responsibilities to her/him as well. Humanity is responsible for protecting all other living things and nature created by Allah (JJH).

When a person believes in Allah (JJH) and makes good deeds, she/he becomes purified as stated in the verse: *But whoever comes before Him a believer having done good deeds, will be raised to higher stations* (20/75). Thus, she/he deserves Paradise (Jannah): *Gardens of Eden [a part of Paradise] with rippling streams, where he will live forever. This is the recompense of those who achieve integrity (purity) (20/76).*

3. The human is honorable but may become reprehensible

In the sight of Allah (JJH), human beings are the most valuable beings. However, her/his spiritual ascent or descent is in her/his own hands. Human *nafs* has some vulnerabilities. According to the Holy Quran, the human is stingy (70/19–21), jealous (4/128), or hasty (21/37, 17/11). Instead of choosing to control her/his own desires in the world and win the hereafter, she/he prefers the pleasures of this world (75/20–21).

The human turns to Allah (JJH) in a difficult situation and forgets Allah (JJH) when the trouble is over. The Holy Quran gives an example from a voyage: *When a calamity befalls you on the sea, all those you invoke fail you except Him. But when He brings you safely to the shore, you turn away, for man is most ungrateful* (17/67). In the Holy Quran, the human is not a static structure but a dynamic being with free will. For this reason, there are both positive and negative descriptions of human beings in the Holy Quran.

4. Since the human has free will to choose good or bad she/he is responsible for the choices and will be recompensed

According to Islam, human beings have a pure inner nature, *fitrah*, which leads to the good. In addition, Allah (JJH) sent prophets and holy books to show people the truth. In the light of both *fitrah* and revealed knowledge the human has the power to distinguish between what is right and wrong: *Surely, We have delivered him to a Way (leading to Allah[JJH]). But either he becomes grateful or ungrateful* (76/3). It is the human being herself/himself who decides her/his own actions by the ability of reason and will power. That is why he/she is responsible for his/her choices and actions. Whether the human chooses the right or wrong she/he will be recompensed in the world and the hereafter: *O humankind! Assuredly there has come to you the truth from your Lord. Whoever, therefore, chooses the right way, follows it but for his own good; and whoever chooses to go astray, goes astray but to his own harm. I am not one appointed as a guardian over you to assume your responsibility* (10/108).

2.2 Descriptions of the Human in the Hadiths of the Prophet Muhammad (PBUH)

In Islam, the holy scripture and the main source of knowledge is the Holy Quran. It is the Prophet Muhammad (PBUH) who explains the verses in the Holy Quran and teaches how to practice them. Therefore, the statements (*hadith*) and actions (*sunnah*) of the Prophet Muhammad (PBUH) are the second main source of knowledge in Islam. While alive, concerned that these sentences might get mixed up with the written verses, he did not let people write down his statements (Musnad, III, 39). Instead, he advised Muslims to memorize his statements and to pass on to others (Abu Dawood, Ilim, 10), which is easier and more trustworthy in a period when written texts were rare, oral literature is effective, and the memories of people were sharp. These Muslims who lived in the period of the Prophet Muhammad (PBUH) were called *ashab* (the companions), and the following generation *tabi'in* (the followers). These two generations began to write the hadith in order not to forget since the Holy Quran was completed and recorded. Then, between the seventh and ninth centuries, Muslims gathered these hadiths and prepared them in a book format. Scholars have classified this process into four stages of memorizing (*hifd*), writing (*kitabat*), collecting (*tadween*), and regimentation (*tasneef*).

Recording the hadith has its own methodology with a unique citation system. A *rawi* (narrator) is a person who memorizes and narrates the sentences of the Prophet Muhammad (PBUH). Ashab, the first generation of Muslims, narrated the sentences of the Prophet Muhammad (PBUH) to the tabi'in, and this transmission of the hadiths has continued for generations. Rawis had not only written the statements of the Prophet Muhammad (PBUH) but also the name of the person who taught to him. Thus, each *riwayah* (statement) has its own citation list. The name list of rawis that reaches the Prophet Muhammad (PBUH) is called *rawi chain*. The more different chains of narrators a hadith has the more robust that hadith is (see Çakan 2016). Today we have such rich hadiths and narrator lists for each. This collection is the second main source of knowledge in Islam.

Since the mission of the Prophet Muhammad (PBUH) is to explain and practice the Holy Quran, his descriptions of the human are also parallel to the verses. He draws attention to the honor of being human and openly stated that people are not superior to each other. In his last sermon of the pilgrimage (*Hajj ul-wida'*), he clearly expressed this: *All mankind is from Adam and Eve, an Arab has no superiority over a non-Arab nor a non-Arab has any superiority over an Arab; also a White has no superiority over a Black nor a Black has any superiority over a White. The superiority only depends on piety and good action in the sight of Allah (JJH)* (Musnad, V, 411).

Pointing at the pure inner nature of the human, he explains the inner voice that tells what is right or wrong as: *Goodness is something that brings peace to the qalb* [heart] *and that makes you relieved. Evil is what makes your qalb restless*

VIEWS OF WESTERN AND ISLAMIC PSYCHOLOGY OF RELIGION

and brings you into doubts, even if people say it's okay (Darimi, Buyu', 2). The Prophet Muhammad (PBUH) makes an emphasis on the qalb and expresses its importance as: *There is a piece of flesh in our body if it is sound the whole body is sound and if it is corrupt the whole body is corrupted. Truly, it is the qalb* (Bukhari, Iman, 39). The importance of the qalb stems from the fact that it is the center of the whole inner world of human beings, such as emotions, thoughts, attitudes, and tendencies, in addition to being the place of real intentions. The Prophet Muhammad (PBUH) says: *Allah looks not at how you look but what is in your hearts and deeds* (Muslim, Birr, 34).

The Prophet Muhammad (PBUH) explained what a great blessing it is for those who wisely use human abilities and free will. In the following hadith, he said that what is important is not the events that happened to those people, but their attitude toward those events: *How pleasant is the situation of the believer. Either way is good for him. This is only for the believer. He is grateful when something good happens to him; that would be good for him. When trouble comes to him, he is patient; that would be good for him as well* (Muslim, Zuhd, 64). He also stated that the human has worldly desires: *If human being had two valleys full of gold, he would like to have the third, for nothing fills his mouth except dust. And Allah (JJH) forgives him who repents to Him* (Muslim, Zakah, 117). So, the human has both worldly desires and higher tendencies and she/he has the chance to be a better or worse person.

A case from the life of Prophet Muhammad (PBUH) summarizes the Islamic understanding of the human. One day, the Prophet Muhammad (PBUH) was traveling with a group of ashab when the camel carrying their food and other necessities ran away. Sa'd b. 'Ubadah, the leader of a prominent family, and his son gave a camel with provisions to the prophet. When the Prophet Muhammad (PBUH) thanked them and gave compliments one of the ashab said that Sa'd had been a good leader before converting as he gave them food during famine. Then the Prophet Muhammad (PBUH) said, *people are like mines. The good ones before Islam are also good people after their conversion to Islam so long as they gain a clear understanding of Islam* (Hanbal, II, 391). This hadith underlines the innate goodness of the human being as Allah does in the Holy Quran.

As a matter of fact, mines are a very good example to explain the human model in Islam. Mines are valuable but they need to be processed to reach their real value. The valuable commodity within the mine exists mixed with worthless materials such as dust, stone, and soil. A diamond needs to be purified to become jewelry. Likewise, human beings have their own cores like gold, silver, emerald, ruby, and so on. Therefore, they need to purify their hearts and develop themselves. Human beings have personal differences and common values in Islam.

2.3 Descriptions of the Human by Muslim Scholars

Following on the Holy Quran and the hadiths of the Prophet Muhammad (PBUH), Muslim scholars have put forth many ideas about the human for centuries. This rich literature of Islamic philosophy contains many correct descriptions that are discussed in psychology today.

Muhasibi (d. 857) is regarded as the first thinker who systematically examined psychological subjects such as states of consciousness, reason, thought, desire, and impulses in the context of the Holy Quran. His ideas were adopted by many subsequent scholars (Hökelekli 2005). According to him, internal experiences can be learned from external observation. He applied the method of introspection to understand and interpret human behavior. Muhasibi, who uses the word 'nafs' in a psychological sense, said that it may tend to be good and evil, so it should be kept under control. He also stated that the desires of the nafs should be fulfilled to some degree (Muhasibi 2009). Thus, Muslim scholars started to develop an Islamic human model in the following centuries.

As their names suggest, the works of Kindi (d. 886) – Al-qawl fi l-nafs (A Treatise on the Nafs), Fi l-'aql (On the Intellect), Mahiyyat an-nawm wa-r-ru'ya (On the Nature of Sleep and Dreams) and al-Hila li-daf'i l-ahzan (The Art of Dispelling Sorrows) – contain psychological perspectives of the ninth century. These works also explain the basic concepts of Islamic psychology. Kindi emphasized that overcoming sadness is possible by changing one's perspective on life, pain, and negativity. This approach is similar to the approach of cognitive psychology today (Gümüşsoy 2018). The demands that emerge under the pressure of basic emotions and passions such as uncontrolled anger and lust, and pathological manifestations such as sadness, anxiety, and fear of death, which are expressions of unhappiness, cause neurotic diseases and hinder moral competence (Kindi 1998). Sadness is a psychological disturbance/sorrow caused by the loss of loved ones/things and unfulfilled requests. The way to get rid of sadness is to gradually learn to deal with it. The basic principle is to accept or impose what is easy to accept first and move toward what is increasingly difficult. Therefore, it can be said that Kindi included the use of cognitive strategies in coping with depression (Köse and Ayten 2012).

Razi (d. 925), another Muslim physician and thinker on psychology, is worth mentioning. His twenty-volume book Kitab ul-hawi fi't-tib (The Comprehensive Book on Medicine) explains his treatment methods, making psychological as well as physiological observations. According to him, the aim of the individual is to pursue knowledge in the world and to strive for eternal happiness (Varlı 2019). He discussed various bad habits and tendencies of the nafs, such as lustful love, self-admiration, envy, lies, stinginess, extreme anger, alcohol addiction, greed, sadness, and fear of death, as well as the relationship of pleasure and sorrow. He also explains their causes, negativities, and what needs to be done to eliminate them (Kaya 2007). Talking about the effects of psychological factors on health, Razi developed the first psychosomatic approach and argued that the troubles of the nafs appear as physiological symptoms in the body (Korkman 2017). Accordingly, he divided medicine into two as physical (*tibb ul-jismani*) and psychological/spiritual (*tibb ur-ruhani*) (Razi 2018). According to him, *tibb ur-ruhani* is the science that protects people from excesses and aims to make them virtuous and happy (Köse and Ayten 2012). Positive suggestion to the patient is a very important method in the treatment of mental/spiritual illnesses. He also mentioned different types of melancholy, hypochondria, the effects of temperament on personality, drowsiness, mental laziness, mental confusion, mental and insomnia diseases, and their treatments (Korkman 2017). These issues are also on the agenda of modern psychology, and Razi's method is similar to suggestopedia.

Adopting Razi's classification of physical and psychospiritual health, Balhi (d. 934) continued to develop an Islamic view in medicine. In his *Masalih ul-abdan wa'l-anfus* (*Sanitation of Body and Nafs*), the chapter on physical health consisted of fourteen sections, including topics such as the need for the protection of the body, the nature of human beings, the formation of organs, eating and drinking habits for health, regular sleep, massage, and physical exercises. The topics of the second chapter, psychospiritual health, include "the ways to protect and regain the health," "emotional ailments and their enumeration," "relieving and controlling anger," "getting rid of fear, sadness and anxiety," and "elimination of delusions and un-controlled thoughts" (Balhi 2022: 191). He stated that the protection of psychospiritual health can take place in two ways: first, avoiding external problems and second, avoiding unrealistic automatic thoughts and cognitive distortions, which are internal processes that will lead to consequences such as excessive sorrow, fear, anger etc. He divided their treatment into two: neurotic disorders that require clinical medical treatment (extrinsic help) and those that require cognitive therapy (intrinsic help). He also defined mental disorders and neurological diseases in four different ways: "fear and worry" (anxiety), "anger and aggression," "sadness and depression," and "obsession and compulsion" (Söylev 2014: 201–202). Additionally, Balhi stated that mental disorders are more common than physical ones, that the degree of being affected by these diseases depends on individual differences, that mental and physical disorders affect each other, and that mental struggles cause physical diseases (Gürsu 2016).

Farabi (d. 950) underlined a new perspective in the tenth century. He explained the importance of the relation between society and the individual in *al-Madinat ul-fadhilah* (*The Virtuous City State*) (Farabi 1997), as social psychology does today. He also mentioned individual psychological issues. To him, qalb is the center of the psychospiritual existence of human. The physical and psychospiritual qalbs interact with each other. The ruh is a spiritual ore, independent of the body. For this reason, the ruh is not affected by death and it exists even if the body dies. *'Aql* (reason/intellect) is the most advanced function of the ruh. 'Aql develops in time and becomes able to comprehend gradually from concrete objects to abstract ideas. This theory is similar to cognitive psychology (Hökelekli 2005).

As a physician who used the methods of observation and experiment, Ibn Sina (d. 1037) dealt with mental as well as physical health and disorders. He explained the causes of many psychotic diseases and pointed to both medication and therapeutic treatments. Similar to the scholars before him, Ibn Sina insisted on the interaction between physical and psychospiritual health. According to him, all biological, physiological, and psychological occurrences in living things are the functions of the ruh/soul. Ibn Sina also argued that the ruh is a self-knowing and therefore body-independent ore. His "flying human" imagery is one of the most effective examples in this regard. According to him, a person who is born in the void and whose body is completely free from external influences, who does not have any knowledge of this world including his own body, that is, who has no perception from the senses, knows his own existence. In this case, the nafs, who knows her/his existence, is a separate gem from the body, and the body is like its dress (Durusoy 1999). The similarity between Ibn Sina's self-knowing nafs and Descartes's "I think therefore I am" is quite remarkable. He further maintained that he had proved the existence of the soul, based on the premise that "All states of consciousness occur in the soul" and "All states of consciousness change, the ruh remains the same" (Taylan 2006). As seen, his ideas that depend on speculation, observation, and experiment contain many subjects related to modern neurobiological psychology, clinical psychology, experimental psychology, cognitive psychology, and mystical psychology.

Ghazali (d. 1111) is one of the most important figures in the history of Islamic thought. His *Ihya' 'ulum ad-din* (*The Revival of Religious Sciences*), *Mukashafat al-qulub* (*Unveiling of Qalbs/Hearts*), *Kimya as-sa'adah* (*The Alchemy of Happiness*), and *al-Munqidh min ad-dalal* (*Rescuer from Error*) are the most cited works in the field of psychology. In particular, the chapter "'Aja'ib al-Qalb"

(Wonders of the Qalb/Heart) in the third volume of *Ihya' 'ulum ad-din* is the most systematic presentation of the concepts of 'qalb,' 'ruh,' 'nafs,' "aql,' and 'fitrah.' That is why Islamic psychology studies mostly refer to him. Ghazali, who deals with the stages that motivate the person to a certain behavior, explained this process as follows: First, a vague feeling occurs in the person. The first thing that enters the area of consciousness is called *khatir* (thought). Then remembering leads to a desire and excitement in the person; this is the stage of *mayl* (inclination). The khatir and mayl are against will, but the next stages occur depending on the will of the person. The desire that is a mayl leads to a judgment in the mind; this process, called "judgment and belief," is the phase of deliberation. The final stage, *niyah* (intention), is the person's decision to take action in order to achieve her/his goal. After the stage of intention, the behavior comes into action. Therefore, the first two of the stages that make up the behavior take place outside of the will. Ghazali argued that in the next stages, the behavior may be stopped before it takes place. According to him, if a person encounters an obstacle in the processes of inclination or intention and believes that she/he should not perform the desired behavior for various reasons, she/he does not display that behavior (Hökelekli 2005). As theory of motivation, Ghazali's theory of personality, and suggestions for recovery from psychological disorders have much in common with today's psychological findings. His views are frequently cited throughout the following as well.

Apart from the above-mentioned scholars, there are plenty of others who discussed psychological issues in Islamic literature, such as Balkhi (d. 934), Ibn Miskawayh (d. 1030), Ibn Hazm (d. 1064), Ibn Tufayl (d. 1118), Ibn Rushd (d. 1198), Ibn 'Arabi (d. 1240), Nasiruddeen al-Tusi (d. 1274), Ibn Qayyim al-Jawziyyah (d. 1350), Ibn Khaldun (d. 1406), Jurjani (d. 1413), Ali Kuşçu (d. 1474), Hocazade Muslihuddin Efendi (d. 1488), Taşköprizade Ahmed Efendi (d. 1561), and Kınalızade Ali (d. 1572). Over time, the Islamic view of the human psyche started to be systematically examined and explained. With accumulation and expansion over time, the Islamic understanding of the human is still effective on Muslim minds.

2.4   *Academic and Institutional Backgrounds of Islamic Psychology*

Islamic civilization has hosted psychological issues at an institutional as well as a scholarly level. Today, the subjects within the field of psychology have been discussed in many disciplines such as morality, *Tasawwuf*,[4] and philosophy.

---

4   Tasawwuf is known as Sufism. But, we prefer to use the term Tasawwuf since the suffix of -ism is used for the ideas of a certain ideology put forward by a group of people. However, tasawwuf is not a human-based school of thought, but a systematic accumulation of Islamic thoughts and practices. See Guénon 1989.

Educational institutions of Islamic civilization have taught these courses from their foundation. Until recently, secondary and higher education centers have generally been expressed with the concept of the madrasah, religious schools built next to the masjid/mosque. In the tenth and eleventh centuries, madrasahs were opened in many cities. The basic curriculum of a madrasah is as follows (Muti 2002: 303–304):

1. Information on the Islamic corpus: Tafsir, hadith, fiqh (Islamic Law).
2. Language and literature lessons: Mainly Arabic.
3. Riaziyyah: Mathematics, geometry, astronomy, algebra, and music.
4. Science of Wisdom: Wisdom (philosophy), logic, knowledge of religions, metaphysics, chemistry, medicine, geography, politics, ethics, and household management. Subjects related to psychology were discussed in the fields of philosophy and medicine.

Apart from these general education institutions, madrasahs were also established for a certain subject, purpose, and service. Three types of madrasah were quite common: The *dar ul-qurra was* specific to the education of reading the Holy Quran, the *dar ul-hadith* was specific to hadith education, and *dar ut-tib* (medical center) to medical education. The first dar ut-tib was established in Damascus in 707 (Hızlı, 1987), showing the importance that Islamic civilization gave to medicine in which psychological disorders were also treated. In 1065, the famous vizier of the Seljuk dynasty, Nizam ul-mulk, built a madrasah called the Nizamiyyah in Baghdad, separated from mosques and allocated only to educating scholars, professors, and statesmen under the control of the state, thus setting a new example for Islamic countries. One of the professors of this madrasah was Ghazali, the famous scholar, philosopher, and educator of the Islamic world in this period (Muti 2002: 300). Thus, academic institutions were founded, in which psychological studies took place as well.

In addition to educational institutions, hospitals were interested in psychology and developed many techniques and treatments for psychological health. For example, physicians appointed to the first dar ut-tib also treated mental disorders and special rooms were built to host the patients with psychological disorders. In addition, hospitals specific to these patients (*bimarhane*) were established in Deynihizkil near Baghdad between 847 and 861, one of the best hospitals of its time, dedicated to the treatment of mental patients only (Hatunoğlu 2014). Then Seljuks, based on the works of Ibn Sina, provided important health services with applied medical schools and educational hospitals in the eleventh and twelfth centuries (Tunaboylu-İkiz 1999). The striking feature of these hospitals is that they trained physicians by providing medical education in addition to hospital services. One of these hospitals was the Gevher Nesibe Medical Madrasah and Hospital, which was opened

VIEWS OF WESTERN AND ISLAMIC PSYCHOLOGY OF RELIGION   27

in 1206 during the Anatolian Seljuk period. This hospital was the first in the world housing both the medical school and the hospital in the same building (Dündar, Emekli, and Şener 2019), just as today's training and research hospitals. Nureddin Hospital, Kayseri Gevher Nesibe Medical Madrasah and Hospital, and Divriği Great Mosque and Hospital had special rooms for clients providing music therapy. They were among the important hospitals of the Seljuks and continued to operate during the Ottoman period (Erer and Atıcı 2010: 30–31).

In the Ottoman understanding of medicine, the idea that "there is a cure for every disease" and that "the cure should be sought" was dominant. The narrations that explain that the Prophet Muhammad (PBUH) opposed those who did not seek a cure for the disease, the belief that the human is the most honorable of the creatures, and the discourse that Allah (JJH) created the cure for all kinds of diseases affected the Ottoman understanding of medicine. Although religious belief shaped the understanding and ethics of medicine, the physician was never seen as a clergyman and was not expected to apply miraculous cures. On the contrary, physicians were regarded as the representatives of the healing of Allah (JJH). It is believed that without the help of Allah (JJH), the patient cannot be cured, no matter how knowledgeable and diligent the physician (Kurtça 2020). Physicians tried to treat both physical and mental disorders. Sufis provide a psychospiritual development process for both healthy people and mental patients. According to Ottoman medical history studies, psychological disorders were being healed in two ways: first is the treatment with methods such as medicine applied by physicians, and the other is the suggested treatment applied by a Sufi leader in a *takkah*, a Sufi center (Tunaboylu İkiz 1999). In other words, medical and mystical practices continued to exist together.

Ottoman hospitals were designed as complex buildings consisting of mosques (masjid), schools (madrasah), soup kitchens (*imarat*), hostels (*tabhanah*), caravansaries (*karwansaray*), baths (*hamam*), bazaars, fountains, and the like. The *dar ush-shifa* (healing center/hospital) is a large complex structure that contains rooms where patients are treated, madrasahs where students receive medical education, places where surgical operations are performed, kitchens where food is cooked for patients, workhouses where drugs are produced, and gardens where the plants to be used in this production are grown (Kurtuluş 2016). Although the Ottoman Empire was not the first civilization that establish dar ush-shifas, it developed the system established by earlier Muslims. Hospitals built during the Ottoman period were (Kurtça 2020): Bursa Yıldırım Dar ush-shifa (1399–1400), İstanbul Fatih Dar ush-shifa (1470), Edirne II. Bayezid Dar ush-shifa (1484–1488), Manisa Hafsa Sultan Dar ush-shifa (1539),

İstanbul Haseki Sultan Dar ush-shifa (1550), İstanbul Suleymaniye Dar ush-shifa (1553–1559), İstanbul-Üsküdar Toptaşı Atik Valide (Nurbânu Sultan) Dar ush-shifa (1582), and İstanbul Sultanahmet Dar ush-shifa (1609–1916). Hospitals were established as a part of the Ottoman foundation (*waqf*) system, and they served without taking any money from the patients. Since the principle of free service to the public was the basis of the complex institutions (*kulliyah*), all these were obliged to provide free services. All services such as accommodation, meals, and other services in caravansaries, treatment, care, and medicines in hospitals, and meals in soup kitchens were provided as a free public service. In these hospitals, where treatment of the poor was the main purpose, no money was taken from the people, and if anyone died there, the burial expenses were also covered (Yıldırım 2014).

One of the basic principles in the treatment of mental patients in the hospitals was for them not to be isolated from physical patients and society. The fact that the Ottomans treated the patients in this way shows that the Ottoman approach to mental illness was not marginalizing. The physical and mental patients were treated together, and hospitals were not far from the city (Kurtuluş 2016). The main practice in the treatment of mental patients in Ottoman society was that the patients were looked after by their families as long as they did not harm the wider society. In the hospitals there were people who showed aggression or were poor and had no one to look after them (Kurtça 2020). There were gradual steps in the treatment process of psychological diseases in these hospitals. The symptoms of the disease were observed first and the most obvious one was highlighted, and the disease was named. Then, the physicians were careful during the illness, and it was believed that the patient was cured when his complaints disappeared, and the patient stopped talking about her/his problems. In the treatment centers, the patient was fed poultry, they watched the landscape, the Holy Quran was read, the sounds of birds and water were listened to, the scents of flowers were enjoyed, and patients were engaged in arts and crafts (Hatunoğlu 2014).

Edirne II. Bayazid Dar ush-shifa was one of the most prominent centers for the different treatment methods in Ottoman hospitals. This hospital has an important place in the history of medicine because of the alternative treatment methods used, especially for mental patients, as well as medical treatments. According to the travel book of Evliya Çelebi (d. 1682), a well-known explorer, every detail was considered for the mental patient, with its foundations, rooms, beds, and garden in the hospital. Besides medical treatments, the sound of water, nature, flowers, and music were also used as a way of treatment. The physicians made the patients listen to music suitable for their temperament, accompanied by *maqam*s suitable for their disorders. In addition, the patients listened to the Holy Quran recitation, *nay* (reed), water, and bird sounds. The patients were also busy with various artistic pursuits in the flower garden of the hospital. Evliya Çelebi mentioned that being hosted on walnut bedsteads with clean sheets in extremely spacious and bright rooms the patients recover in a short time (Özkaya 2016).

As stated in the 1490 foundation charter of Edirne Dar ush-shifa, it was established as a hospital where doctors from different branches served the city's healthcare needs. For this reason, people suffering from all kinds of diseases were treated in this hospital. However, this situation began to change at the end of the eighteenth century and intensely in the nineteenth century, when the hospital became a place where the mental patients were isolated. The removal of these patients from Edirne Dar ush-shifa and the complete loss of function of the hospital came in 1915 when Dr. Mazhar Osman, who is accepted as the founder of modern Turkish psychiatry, unchained about forty mentally ill people, five of whom were women. These patients were isolated in chains in Edirne Hospital and Osman took them to İstanbul Toptaşı Hospital. Thus, this important hospital, where according to its foundation charter twenty-one personnel worked for forty patients, and mental patients were treated with alternative methods such as music, water sound, and plants, and fed with menus specially prepared by doctors, was completely closed in 1915, becoming a neglected place where patients were isolated (Kurtça 2020). Today the hospital building is an open-air museum.

In summary, it can be said that the Islamic literature contains many descriptions of the subjects that today fall under the field of psychology. The views of Muslim scholars on the human psyche, which have accumulated over the centuries, not only remained in theory but also have shaped practice. Educational institutions that deal with psychological issues and health centers that offer treatment for psychological disorders have been established throughout the Islamic world. Thus, the Islamic view of the human has survived to the present day. However, psychology based on Western human understanding also existed simultaneously. With the encounter of these two approaches, a specific field called Islamic psychology has started to be mentioned.

3 How to Combine Western and Islamic Psychologies

As presented in the first chapter, Western psychology was founded in 1879 in Germany. Departments of psychology and psychiatry were then established in several universities in Europe and America. Psychological theories, research, and therapy techniques emerged and publications on these three continue up to the present. Non-Western countries met this new approach to the human via translations, the Western scholars who traveled to these countries, and their own scholars who traveled to Western countries at the very beginning of the emergence of the discipline.

Non-Western countries mostly have an understanding of the human within their thought systems and they have mental health practices based on their religious and cultural backgrounds. Mental health services may also be provided through doctors, clergy, or magicians by traditional practices such as shrine visiting. It is a natural reaction of these cultures to compare their theory and practices about the human when they encounter a new approach such as Western psychology. In general, non-Western countries imported psychology that emerged in the West at the end of the nineteenth century and the beginning of the twentieth century. Although these psychology studies have attracted attention in almost all non-Western countries, there have been some challenges at the theory, research, and practice level in their culture. Even the papers presented in the history of psychology section of the International Psychology Congress (ICP) held in South Africa in 2012 indicate that psychological research and practices in non-Western countries need to be harmonized with the cultural and religious codes of that country (Brock et al. 2012). Many researchers from different parts of the world, such as Ghana (Asante 2012), Cuba (Reyes and Moreno 2012), Tunisia (Bellaj 2012), Algeria (Mebarki 2012), India (Verma, Khan, and Subba 2012), and Japan (Igarashi 2012) expressed the difficulties experienced in explaining daily life of their own countries with European and American-based psychology. They also emphasized the necessity of developing local psychological approaches and producing solutions to psychological problems. In this context, Islamic countries have also taken into account their traditional knowledge of the human while working within this new discipline. Although Islamic countries are culturally diverse, they have the same belief in the background of their cultures. Therefore, the viewpoint of these cultures on the human also has many common points. The beginning of the study of Western psychology in Muslim majority countries was the first contact between Western and Islamic psychologies.

3.1 The Contact between Western and Islamic Psychologies

The first contact between Western and Islamic psychologies took place in the Ottoman Empire, the closest Islamic area to Europe. The years when psychology was established in Europe, correspond to the last periods of the Ottoman Empire. Psychology lectures were given in Ottoman educational institutions under the names "'ilm un-nafs," "ruhiyyat," or "'ilm-i ahwal-i ruh" (Kılıç 2015), and there were fully equipped hospitals that offered specialized treatment for

VIEWS OF WESTERN AND ISLAMIC PSYCHOLOGY OF RELIGION 31

psychological diseases via music therapy, art therapy, and so on. These lectures and practices were based on the understanding of the human in Islamic literature. Since the Ottoman Empire was in a period of renewal at the turn of the twentieth century, Ottoman scholars also studied the views of scholars in Europe at the point when claims were made that psychology should be a separate discipline in Europe.

The first psychology book that also discussed the Western approach was dated 1878, before the official establishment of the psychology laboratory in the University of Leipzig (Bilgin 1988). In *Gayet'ül Beyan fi Hakikat'il-İnsan yahut İlm-i Ahval-i Ruh* (*An Attempt to Express the Essence of Human Being or The States of Soul/Spirit-Psychology*), Yusuf Kemal claimed that the body of a human is explained by medicine and anatomy, and her/his spiritual/psychological nature such as attitudes, behaviors, feelings, and thoughts by the term *'ilm-i ahwal-i ruh* (psychology), revealing the difference of this field from the fields of *'ilm-i kalam* (theology), *mantiq* (logic) and *'ilm-i tehzip* (morality). Frequently referring to European thinkers such as Leibniz, the author considers 'ilm-i ahwal-i ruh as a separate field within the branches of philosophy. The psychological topics such as conscience, power of feeling, power of acting, power of comprehending, senses, understanding, imagination, and memory are discussed in the book. Additionally, the interaction between the ruh (soul/spirit) and the nafs (self/psyche) is also discussed, and the proofs from the verses of the Holy Quran regarding the immortality of the soul and the existence of the hereafter are also put forth.

Although Yusuf Kemal's book is accepted as the first psychology book in the Ottoman Empire, the historical sources also show that the first psychology book was actually written earlier. Hasan Tahsin, known as Hodja Tahsin, stated that he wrote *İlm-i Ahval-i Ruh* around 1873, however it was not published until after his death, by his student in 1892. Hodja Tahsin was sent to Paris in 1873 to study science in order to give lectures at the newly established dar ul-funun, an educational institution, in İstanbul (Akün 1998). The dar ul-funun was designed differently from other educational institutions such as madrasahs. The lexical meaning of dar ul-funun is "the house of science, mainly natural sciences." While some parts of the building were still under construction, lectures in physics, chemistry, history, geography, and natural science began to be given to the public in the completed parts in 1863. This institution was designed as three faculties: philosophy and literature, law, and natural sciences and mathematics (İhsanoğlu 1993). Hodja Tahsin was appointed as the head of the faculty of natural sciences and mathematics. This institution is considered the first modern university that included Western ideas such as positivism and humanism, with a library and graduate programs (Horozcu 2010). The first known lecture on psychology at the university level was "Amjaz-i Akaleem" (Temperaments of Climates), which Aziz Efendi gave among his public lectures in 1869, before the official opening of the institution in 1870. It is known that after the 1908 revolution, Babanzade Naim also gave some theology-oriented psychology courses under the name of "'ilm un-nafs" in this school (Batur 2003). In these books and lectures, Western and Islamic understandings coexisted. The list of psychology publications sheds light on the historical background of the contact of Western and Islamic psychologies (Table 2).

These publications include information about both the human understanding of the Islamic tradition and the view of Western science on human beings. For example, in his first statement on the neurological structure of the brain, Rıfat b. Mehmed Emin stated that thought occurs through chemical reactions emerging in the nerves. However, he did not neglect to add that only Allah (JJH) knows the real mystery of thought (Gözütok 2013). Traces of Islamic and Western psychology appear together in the psychology studies written at that

TABLE 2   First psychology books in Ottoman Turkish

Author	Year	Title
Yusuf Kemal Bey	1878	*Gâyet'ül-Beyân fî Hakîkat-i İnsân yahut İlm-i Ahval-i Ruh* [*An Attempt to Express the Essence of Human Being or the States of Soul/Spirit*]
Ahmed Midhat	1881	*Nevm ve Hâlât-ı Nevm* [*Dreams and the States of Dreams*]
Sırrı Giridi	1885	*Ruh* [*Soul/Spirit/Psyche*]
Ahmed Midhat	1885	*İlhâmât ve Tağlitât. Psikoloji, yani Fenn-i Menâfi'ü'r-Rûha Dâ'ir Bazı Mülâhâzât* [*Inspirations and Deceptions: Some Thoughts on Psychology, the Science of the Functions of Soul/Spirit/Psyche*]
Hoca Tahsin	1892	*Psikoloji Yâhûd İlm-i Ahvâl-i Rûh* [*Psychology or Ilm-i Ahwal-i ruh*]
Mehmet Fahri	1892	*Hıfz-ı Sıhhat-i İşgâlât-ı Zihniyye* [*Protection of Mental Activity Health*]
Rıfat b. Mehmed Emin	1893	*İlm-i Ahvâl-i Rûh ve Usûl-i Tefekkür* [*Ilm-i Ahwal-i Ruh and The Methodology of Thought*]

SOURCE: BELEN 2019: 74

VIEWS OF WESTERN AND ISLAMIC PSYCHOLOGY OF RELIGION

TABLE 3   Significant translated psychology books in Ottoman Turkish

Author	Year	Title	Translator
G. Le Bon	1907	*Ruh'ul Akvam* [*Spirit (Psychology) of Folks/Communities*]	Abdullah Cevdet
A. Binet and T. Simon	1915	*Çocuklarda Zekânın Mikyâsı* [*The Development of Intelligence in Children*]	İ. Alaaddin (Gövsa)
G. Le Bon	1918	*Avrupa Harbinden Alınan Psikolociya-i Dersler* [*Psychological Lessons Taken from the European War*]	Abdullah Cevdet
W. James	1919	*İtiyât* [*Habit*]	Mustafa Rahmi (Balaban)
H. Høffding	1924	*Tecrübe Üzerine Müesses Psikoloji* [*Psychology Depended on Experience*]	Hüseyin Cahit (Yalçın)

SOURCE: BELEN 2019: 75

time. Translations also increased in the same period (see Table 3), thus, the Western psychological approach to the human was published without mentioning the Islamic or cultural background.

As seen, approaches to psychology in Europe were brought into Ottoman Turkish in a very short time. Translations, lectures, and publications on psychology show that scholars in the Ottoman Empire and Türkiye stayed abreast of the journey of psychology to become an independent discipline in Europe. For example, the Binet-Simon intelligence test was adapted to Türkiye in 1915, one year before it was adapted to the United States. Thus, it is possible to say that the first contact of Western psychology and Islamic understanding was almost simultaneous with the scientific transformation in Europe.

Some histories of psychology sources attribute the foundation of experimental psychology in Türkiye – without mentioning the Islamic background – to 1915, when German researcher Georg Auschütz came to İstanbul to teach psychology at the dar ul-funun. He considered psychology as an experimental science and brought some experimental instruments with him. Since only a few students graduated from the university in those years due to the war, the psychological education was not very active, and more generally he was busy with his own studies (Batur 2003). However, his contributions to psychology in

İstanbul were limited as, like all German academics, he returned to Germany at the end of World War I in 1918. This limited contribution was not seen as the establishment of scientific psychology in the Ottoman Empire and Türkiye.

It is generally accepted that the foundation of scientific psychology in Türkiye is based on the establishment of the general psychology department at İstanbul University in 1919. The pioneer of psychology in Türkiye is Mustafa Şekip Tunç, who founded and chaired this department after studying at the Geneva J.J. Rousse Institute. He published *Ruhiyat Dersleri* (*Psychology Lectures*) in the same year and began to give psychology classes. Then, invited to Türkiye from England, Prof. Wilhelm Peters founded the experimental psychology department and pedagogy institute in 1937, establishing a psychology library and laboratory in İstanbul with his colleague Mümtaz Turhan (Kılıç 2015; Toğrol 1987).

While the development of the psychology department at the university level continued, the teaching of psychology courses in theology departments also came to the fore. The Dar ul-funun u Shahane was established in İstanbul in 1900, and faculties of literature and philosophy, mathematics and natural sciences, and religious sciences were opened. Philosophy and psychology courses were not included in the curriculum of theology in the first semester, but in 1912, it was decided to provide an 'ilm un nafs course for the second-year undergraduate students, but this course was not taught due to various institutional difficulties. Besides, the Madrasah al-Mutahasseseen was opened in 1914 within the scope of the law of renewal of madrasahs. In this institution, whose name was changed to Suleymaniye Madrasah four years later, Tasawwuf, 'ilm un-nafs, and morality were taught in the first grade within the theology and philosophy courses (Horozcu 2009). After the establishment of the Republic of Türkiye, state institutions were restructured, and universities began to be opened that provided psychology and psychology of religion courses.

A dar ul-funun was established in 1908 in Egypt, which was officially affiliated to the Ottoman State at that time. Later, the name of this institution was changed from the University of Egypt to the University of Cairo. This institution sent researchers to England, France, and later to the United States to study modern sciences. French professors gave the first psychology courses at this university, and the first known psychology conference in Egypt was given in 1911. The psychology department, which was placed under the philosophy department, was the responsibility of Yusuf Murad, who had a doctorate in experimental psychology in France (Ibrahim 2013; Mohamed 2012).

Iran, another prominent Islamic country during this period, experienced a similar process to the Ottoman Empire. Historians attribute the beginning of modern psychology in Iran to the lecture "'Ilm un-nafs and Education" given by Ali Akbar Siassi at the Academy of Politics in 1925. Siassi, based on the lessons he gave, published *Psychology or 'Ilm un-Nafs in Terms of Education* and *Fundamentals of Psychology* in 1938 (Hosseingholizadeh 2013). With his efforts, the first psychology laboratory was established in 1935. Tehran University's medical faculty also started to teach a course called psychiatry methods in 1937, and the first psychology department was established in 1963 (Anbari, Baranovich, and Zailaini 2019). Published in 1954 by Siassi, *Avicenna's Ilm un-Nafs and Its Comparison with New Psychology*, is an example for utilizing both sources by the thinkers of Islamic countries who encounter Western psychology. Anbari, Baranovich, and Zailaini also underline the need to consider the Western and Islamic perspectives together in psychology studies in Iran: "Psychology as a major is a new identity that seeks to integrate three different subjects in Iran, commitment to religion and Islamic philosophy, use of new and international methods and approaches, and meeting the present needs of Iranian people" (2019: 788).

Other Muslim regions have a similar history of psychology. A department of psychology was established in the Government College of Lahore in 1932 where Muhammad Iqbal wrote *The Reconstruction of Islamic Thought* in 1930. He developed his own theory of self (*khudi/nafs*) from an Islamic perspective while discussing the thoughts of Kant, Hegel, Goethe, Freud, and James. Because of geographical distance and political reasons other countries started to study Western psychology after the 1950s. For instance, the psychology faculty was established at Padjadjaran University in 1961 in Indonesia, and in 1974 psychology courses were given at the University of Malaya in Malaysia (Ayten and Hussain, 2020). Thus, the Western view of human encountered the Islamic one in all Muslim regions.

Psychology and psychology of religion developments are simultaneous, both institutionally and in publications in Islamic countries as in the West. The figures who undertook the first psychology studies in Türkiye also discussed religious issues. For example, Mustafa Şekip Tunç, who is considered to be the founder of modern psychology in Türkiye, published an article in 1953 titled "Mysticism and Sufis," dealing with mysticism in general and Tasawwuf in particular, in addition to many original and translated psychology studies. In *Towards a Philosophy of Religion* (1959), Mustafa Şekip Tunç explicitly mentioned the psychology of religion as a field. He stated that the most intense experiences of the human are religious experiences and that this experience should be examined from a psychological point of view. He drew attention to the importance of religious experience, religious feeling, and religious consciousness, and conducted studies not only in general psychology but also in the psychology of religion (Arıcan 2006). It should be noted that the examination of the components of Turkish-Islamic culture in terms of Western modern psychology goes back earlier. The first studies that used the terms religion and psychology together belong to Hilmi Ziya Ülkenin two articles published in 1924, "Religious Spirituality/Psychology Observations in Anatolian History: Burak Baba, Geyikli Baba" and "Religious Spirituality/Psychology Observations in Anatolian History: Haji Baktash Wali." In these articles, Ülken examined three Sufis in Anatolian history in terms of neuropathy, based on the views of William James.

The field that presents human feelings, thoughts, and behaviors in the most systematic way in the Islamic tradition is Tasawwuf. The experiences and thoughts of the famous Sufis still inspire people. For this reason, it is a natural result that Muslim scholars who encounter studies in the field of psychology in Europe, mostly referred to Tasawwuf. Ülken was the first person to use the term "psychology of tasawwuf" by pointing to this fact. In 1946 he published a short book, *Psychology of Tasawwuf*, comparing the human model of Islamic Tasawwuf with the approaches of scholars such as Freud, Adler, and Janet. His following words shed light on the contact of Western and Islamic psychologies:

> Modern psychology is undoubtedly established without taking into account the oldest experiences in human history. Its foundations are today's life, laboratories, hospitals, schools, and today's technique of investigation and treatment. It even has to ignore what the ancients did in order to protect itself from all kinds of preconceptions and wrong thoughts in its own research. For this reason, no matter how suspicious they regard the existence and attainments of the experiences before science, these new ways of psychology should not be considered completely false. Especially those who work in positive, experiential, or rational ways should avoid the movements with clearly mystical methods and aims. However, after these researches are done, there is nothing more natural than making such a comparison. What we are looking for in such a comparison of the experience of the Sufis is not the roots of scientific truths, but the roots of theological truths but the roots of psychological experiences that scholars have reached.
>
> ÜLKEN 1946: 205

In sum, it can be stated that both psychology and psychology of religion in Türkiye have studied Western psychological views as well as continued to study religious and cultural understandings of the human. In an article where he wrote his evaluations of psychology studies in Türkiye, Fred McKinney, who had been to Türkiye for a while, stated that young people were under Islamic-European influences (McKinney 1960). Although there have been great changes since then, the Western and Islamic approaches to the human have coexisted.

Today, there are four different types of department related to psychology in Türkiye: *psychiatry* departments in medical faculties; *psychology* divisions in the faculties of science and literature; departments of *psychological counseling and guidance* in education faculties; and *psychology of religion* departments in the faculties of theology. Except from psychology of religion departments, these are largely based on Western psychology, and until recently did not publish much on subjects related to religion or spirituality.

The first theology faculty in Türkiye was opened in Ankara University in 1949 and the psychology of religion course was included in the curriculum (Ayhan 2000), with the psychology of religion department opening and courses taught since then. Today, the curriculum of theology faculties in Türkiye is different from the departments of Islamic studies in other countries, most of which are limited to basic Islamic studies There are three main departments within theology faculties in Türkiye. First is the main department of *basic Islamic sciences*, which includes departments such as *tafsir* (Quranic commentary), hadith, and Islamic law. Second is the main department of *Islamic history and arts*, which includes departments such as Islamic arts and aesthetics, Islamic history, and religious music. Third is the main department of *philosophy and sciences/studies of religion*, which includes departments such as psychology of religion, sociology of religion, and philosophy of religion. All these departments have their own masters and PhD programs. The psychology of religion department has been teaching scientific methods of psychology as well as the Islamic view of the human and producing publications for seventy-two years. This model is a good example for the training of Islamic psychology researchers familiar with Islamic literature and scientific psychology.

3.2   *Islamic Psychology and Sufi Psychology*

Psychology has founded subbranches dealing with many different subjects over time, and the psychology of religion has continued to exist as one of these. On the other hand, the religious psychology approach has always existed within the psychology of religion studies. Since the science of psychology emerged in the West, studies of the psychology of religion were generally based on Christianity. Therefore, Christian psychology has come to the fore in the approach of religious psychology. Over time, studies such as Hindu psychology, Buddhist psychology, and Jewish psychology have taken their place in the literature.

As part of the zeitgeist, Muslim majority countries have undertaken studies that deal with Western psychology theories and methods together with the human understanding of Islam since the time they encountered scientific psychology. However, most of these publications reached local readers only as they were published in the local language, as mentioned above. Consequently, these were not known in Europe and America as they remained untranslated. Haque (1998) suggests that the studies of the Arabs are not known by the West because they are not translated into English, but this is also true for other Muslim countries. Issues such as language differences and difficulty in accessing information were also slowing down the interaction between Muslim countries. Once Islam-centered psychology studies began to be published in English and it became easier to share information with the help of technological developments, Muslim psychologists started to cooperate more with both Western and other Muslim psychologists, and the concept of Islamic psychology began to be used clearly.

Sources date the beginning of Islamic psychology to the 1950s–1970s, and names such as Muhammed Qutb, Malik Badri, and Uthman Najati (Ayten and Hussain 2020; Iqbal and Skinner 2021; Uysal 2021). This may be true when talking about the Islamic psychology movement, but it should not be forgotten that the first Islamic psychology studies discussing, adopting, and criticizing Western psychology go back to the 1870s. English seems to have provided Muslims a common language because, even among Muslim countries, the literature on Islamic psychology is English based. For example, those who collect and classify Islamic psychology studies only look at English sources (Abu Raiya 2013; Haque et al. 2016), but there are many more theoretical, research, and application-based studies on Islam and psychology in Arabic, Turkish, Persian, Urdu, Indonesian, and Malaysian literatures. Almost all psychology of religion studies in Muslim countries are related to Islam/Muslims and include an Islamic psychology approach. It would be an important attempt to systematically bring this corpus to the English literature by a committee from Muslim countries. Here, we will only touch on the field of Islamic psychology.

Over time, theories based on the Islamic understanding of the human and empirical research with a Muslim sample have increased so much that they constitute a serious amount in the literature. These studies have revealed the aspects of psychological theory, research, and practices originating from the West, as well as revealing the characteristic ways of thinking, feeling, and behaving of Muslim minds. This literature also includes issues such as the nature of religion, conversion, spirituality, and atheism (Sevinç, Coleman, and Hood 2018), among others.

As in the psychology of religion studies in the West, the psychology of religion approach and the religious psychology approach coexisted in the psychology of religion studies in Islamic countries. A distinction between psychology of Islam and Islamic psychology (Uysal 2021) comes to the fore just as the distinction between psychology of Christianity and Christian psychology. The psychological research with a Muslim sample can be regarded psychology of Islam (Abu Raiya 2013), while psychological studies based on Islamic thought can be regarded as Islamic psychology. Moreover, this classification can be specialized to psychology of Tasawwuf as a subbranch of psychology of Islam and Sufi psychology as a subbranch of Islamic psychology. So, Islamic psychology is not limited to a psychology of Muslims. Rather, it is an explanation of the human with a long history and a new approach for psychological studies depending on Islamic teachings.

For now, there has not been a clear distinction between psychology of Islam and Islamic psychology, and they are used interchangeably. However, the subjects studied under the title of psychology and Islam in general (Ayten and Hussain 2020; Iqbal and Skinner 2021) will gain clearer classifications soon since attempts to define the field of Islamic psychology are rapidly growing in the literature.

Today, as a new paradigm, Islamic psychology (Khodayarifard et al. 2021) attracts attention all over the world. Some developments in psychology studies in Europe and America paved a way for Islamic psychology to come to the fore, like other religious psychologies. The first factor is large-scale international research. The recent results of these studies revealed that although the rates of happiness (average life evaluation) are not high in Muslim countries in the *World Happiness Report* (Helliwell et al. 2021), suicide rates are lower in the *World Health Statistics* (WHO 2021). In addition, it has been found that an Islamic-centered understanding is dominant in the basic issues of psychology, such as meaning in life and coping, in Muslim countries (Abu Raiya 2013; Ayten 2018; Ayten et al., 2012; Göcen 2012, 2013; Karagöz 2020; Vural and Ayten 2022). These findings aroused interest in the psychological effects of the teachings of Islam.

The second factor that is effective in bringing Islamic psychology to the agenda is the general acceptance of the idea that human beings have a spiritual as well as a physical, mental, and social dimension. The changing of the definition of 'health' by the World Health Organization (1998) has also accelerated spirituality studies. In the West, religion and spirituality began to be handled as separate phenomena, and religion and spirituality were explained through individual experiences. The absence of such an institution in Islam – like the church in Christianity – did not allow this distinction to be made very sharply in Muslim countries.

Studies have revealed that Muslims code religion and spirituality in close places in their minds (Altınlı-Macic and Coleman, 2015; Düzgüner 2021; Khodayarifard et al. 2021; Rahnama et al. 2012). For example, concepts such as god, transcendent being, supreme power, and ultimate being all evoke Allah (JJH) for Muslims. So, spirituality, which is defined as the relationship with the higher being, also means being in a relationship with Allah (JJH) (Düzgüner 2021). Therefore, spirituality in Muslim minds includes actions such as five-times-a-day prayer, reading the Holy Quran, fasting during Ramadan, and giving zakat, which are ways of establishing a relationship with Allah (JJH). In addition, actions such as helping others, hiking, and listening to music are examples of spirituality, but for Muslims, these actions also have a spiritual character as they remind them of Allah (JJH). Hiking means admiring the beauties created by Allah (JJH); the verses of *think about the creation of heaven and earth* in the Holy Quran (3/191) show that spending time in nature is a kind of religious behavior and worship in Islam. Meditation or the exercise of focusing on the inner world all alone is like *tafakkur* (contemplation) in Islam. There are many verses in the Holy Quran on making tafakkur about Allah (JJH) (30/8; 39/42; 59/21; 45/13). The worship of *i'tikaf*, which is performed in mosques or homes in the last ten days of Ramadan, also depends on the remembrance of Allah (JJH) by focusing on the inner world of the individual. Therefore, for Muslim minds, tafakkur – namely meditating – is not separate from the remembrance of Allah (JJH). Moreover, the verse *They remember Allah (JJH) while standing, sitting and lying down* (3/191) indicates that a Muslim is not only in a relationship with Allah (JJH) while hiking, praying, or contemplating but every single moment. The spread of spirituality in psychology and the use of spiritual well-being as a psychological term brought the spiritual world of Muslims to the agenda, which directly opened the door to Islamic psychology. At this point, it should be noted that for Muslims, spirituality is not a purely religious phenomenon, but in Muslim minds, religion and spirituality are perceived more intertwined than in the West since Islam is both worship and experience-based religion (see Düzgüner 2021).

The third factor effective on the interest toward Islamic psychology is Western curiosity to Eastern traditions. Spirituality – far from institutional religion – started to be experienced through yoga and meditation, and a tendency toward New Age movements increased in Western countries. Then, aromatherapies, effective stones, yoga meditation sessions, spiritual life coaching, aura, and chakras have taken their place in daily language and practices in different cultures and religions. Many Western people have started to perform yoga and meditation while they do not attend church services at all. We have observed that yoga and meditation performers in America were more numerous than those in Japan which has a Far Eastern culture. The sentence "I am spiritual but not religious" is getting expressed more loudly in the West. In this tendency to spirituality, the ideas of the mystics like Gandhi, Confucius, and Rumi have attracted more attention. So, Islam and Tasawwuf, as well as Far Eastern traditions, have aroused interest recently by insisting on personal transcendence experiences.

The fourth factor that has recently emerged in the field of psychology and has enabled the discussion of Islamic psychology is the fact that many studies have revealed the relationship between religiosity/spirituality and mental health. Subsequently it has been demonstrated by scientific studies that religious/spiritual care/counseling is effective in the treatment process of psychological – even physical – diseases (Ayten 2018; Ayten et al. 2012; Göcen 2012, 2016; Koenig 2016). Thus, religion and spirituality began to be talked about more in the field of psychology, and religious support was included among patients' rights (World Medical Association 1981). Considering the religious and spiritual support in health practices all over the world, it is a natural result that Islam, the second-largest religion in the world, has attracted attention in psychology studies.

The fifth factor effective in bringing Islamic psychology to the agenda can be summarized as pluralism. Psychological support services had to be developed according to people from different backgrounds in metropolises where groups of people from different cultures live together. It has been argued that Islam-centered meaning-making and coping strategies will be effective in approaching Muslim clients (Abu Raiya and Pargament 2010; Hamdan 2007).

The interest in Islamic psychology depends on the zeitgeist in the West, which emerged as a result of these factors. Islamic literature touches psychological issues in different fields, most of which belong to Tasawwuf. In Sufi sources, there are deep analyses on human nature, inner world, perceptions, attitudes, personality, and many applications for the spiritual development of human beings. Moreover, these theories and practices are not only the product of thought (speculation) but also the result of research and practice over centuries (Ülken 1946). The most detailed and systematic explanations of psychological phenomena belong to the Sufi leaders. Even today, the thoughts and practices of great Sufis such as Mawlana Jalaluddeen Rumi, Yunus Emre, and Ahmad Yasawi are well known by Muslims and shape the minds of the public. For instance, in Pew's 2012 international survey about Muslim diversity (Pew 2012), Turkish people replied "yes" much more often than the other

Muslim majority countries to the question "is devotional dancing acceptable?" just because they regard the question related to whirling dervishes ceremonies that depend on Rumi. These ceremonies are considered very spiritual, mystical, and religious by the attendees (Düzgüner 2013b), and the ceremonies still attract attention all over the world as well as the ideas of great Sufis. This is an example to show how sufi teachings and practices are effective on Mulsim minds. Accordingly, the intersections of Tasawwuf with psychology are of interest (Küçük 2009; Merter 2014; Sayar 2010; Tarhan 2013). For this reason, a field of 'Sufi psychology' is in the process of being formed under the title of Islamic psychology.

Here, we come up with the definitions of the above-mentioned fields as:
- *Psychology of religion* is a wide field that examines the reflections of belief and unbelief to the life of an individual through psychological research methods.
- *Religious psychology* consists of psychological studies based on a certain religion such as Buddhist psychology, Christian psychology, and Islamic psychology.
- *Islamic psychology* is a field that investigates psychological issues based on Islamic thought.
- *Sufi psychology* is a field that investigates psychological issues based on Sufi teachings.

In this case, we assert a series of research fields from general to specific: psychology – psychology of religion – religious psychology – Islamic psychology – Sufi psychology (Figure 2). The initial steps of the presented model

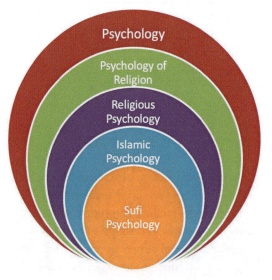

FIGURE 2
From general to specific psychological research areas
SOURCE: AYTEN AND DÜZGÜNER 2017: 45

(psychology – psychology of religion – religious psychology) are suitable for classifying studies all over the world. As we assert Islamic psychology – Sufi psychology, the model can then continue on the basis of religious teaching and continue with a more specific field of study within a specific religion, such as Jewish psychology – Kabbalah psychology, or Buddhist psychology – yoga psychology. Although the boundaries between these areas are not very clear, the literature of psychology of religion has reached a saturation that will enable this general classification. We believe that the model is functional in the studies of psychology of religion.

The first studies on psychology of religion in Türkiye are a good example of this model. The first Turkish study was *Psychology of Religion: An Attempt on the Field, Sources, and Method*, written by Bedii Ziya Egemen in 1952. Then Osman Pazarlı in 1968 and Turgut İ. Ulusoy in 1970 both wrote books with the same title, *Psychology of Religion*. These books that outline the scope of psychology of religion, in general, include the history, subjects, and methods of psychology of religions as well as the topics related to Islam and Tasawwuf. So, these books show that both Western and Islamic psychologies of religion were featured in the earliest studies containing both psychology of religion and religious psychology approaches. Belma Özbaydar's (1970) study, *Research on the Development of Belief in Religion and God*, was the first survey conducted on the psychology of religion in Türkiye. *Religious Symptoms in Psychopathology*, by Neda Armaner in 1973, determines the boundaries of pathological and religious behavior. These books are examples of psychology of religion without an Islamic or Sufi perspective.

On the other hand, Mehmet Tevfik, a specialist at the Bakırköy Mental and Neurological Diseases Hospital, wrote *Psychological Depressions and Islamic Spirituality* in 1975. He discusses Western psychology under the light of the Holy Quran and Sunnah. Likewise, written by the first professors of the departments of psychology of religion in universities, *Writings of Islamic Psychology* (Hökelekli 2010) and *Worship Psychology: The Case of Prophet Muhammad* (Şentürk 2008) can be considered as Islamic psychology. *Sufi Psychology* (Sayar 2010) and *Nafs Psychology* (Merter 2014) written by psychiatrists, as well as *Psychology of Tasawwuf* (Kayıklık 2011b) and *Introduction to Psychology of Tasawwuf* (Ayten and Düzgüner 2017) written by scholars of the psychology of religion can be considered as Sufi psychology since the writers present the Sufi perspectives on the issues. A glance at the topics of publications of the psychology of religion in Türkiye alone (Sevinç 2013; Güven and Güven 2021) shows the richness of the field and the validity of the model.

3.3 Sensitive Points in Studying Islamic Psychology

Although the subjects related to psychology and Islam have gained interest recently, these studies were not easily accepted and rapidly developed. The challenges and sensitive points to be considered in Islamic psychology studies are as follows.

3.3.1 Denial of Psychology

When Muslim countries meet with Western psychology, they give various reactions. Although some scholars study psychology, others deny this science. They argue that the Islamic approach is sufficient to understand the human and to find solutions to her/his problems. They reject Western psychology completely. This approach is called the exclusive path by Ayten and Hussain (2020: 32). Because of this belief, some people prefer to go to an imam or a religious leader rather than a psychologist when they have psychological problems. To this attitude, a person should review her/his religious life when she/he has psychological problems, which will be discussed later. The fear of being stigmatized as "crazy" for going to a psychologist is also effective on this attitude. So, this approach is purely theology-based and ignores psychology. Therefore, these scholars do not accept the field of Islamic psychology either.

3.3.2 Disregard of Religion/Islamic View in Psychology

There are also scholars in Muslim countries who adopt the scientific positivistic psychology approach and exclude the determinations of religions about human beings from the field of study (Badri 2016; Hökelekli 2016) as many Western psychologists do. Unlike academics and psychologists in Europe and America, some psychologists in Muslim countries generally exclude the concept of religion from their interest completely. This attitude comprises adopting a strict positivist paradigm and avoiding all religious sources. For this reason, they reject not only Islamic psychology but also the psychology of religion. For example, while Freud's theories and psychoanalysis are taught in many psychology departments, including those in Türkiye, his books on religion such as *Moses and Monotheism* are not mentioned. It is not even acknowledged that the APA has a division for psychology of religion and spirituality. Since the psychology of religion departments in Türkiye are in faculties of theology, the departments of psychology, psychiatry, and psychological counseling often ignore such a field. Even though they know otherwise, they consider it as theology, not a subbranch of psychology (Ertürk 2017).

3.3.3 Superficial Approach

This approach focuses on the psychological benefits of religious practices, disregarding their religious meaning. Some Buddhists are critical that yoga and meditation were secularized and separated from the spiritual tradition in Western applications today. Islamic practices have the potential to contribute in the same way (York Al-Karam 2018) but it is against the Islamic spirit. For instance, fasting during Ramadan has a positive effect on physical health but a Muslim does not fast to be fit and healthy; if so, it is not worship but a diet. Likewise, Islamic beliefs and practices have a positive effect on psychological well-being, but psychological health is not the only and ultimate goal in Islam. It is necessary to investigate the psychological functions of religion and spirituality in academic studies. However, the functions of religion are not the religion itself. A researcher may adopt a functional approach to the subject, but she/he cannot disregard the substantive dimension of Islam.

3.3.4 Confusion of Concepts

There are many concepts and definitions in the descriptions of the human in Islamic literature, starting from the Holy Quran and hadiths up to the present. The concepts that are in the field of psychology today form the basis of Islamic psychology. At the beginning of these are the concepts of ruh (soul, spirit) and nafs (self, psyche). While some sources use these two synonymously, others use them with different meanings (Khodayarifard et al. 2021). On the other hand, the usage and definitions of concepts such as 'aql (intellect, reason), qalb (heart/mind), fitrah (pure nature) vary even in Muhasibi, Ghazali, and Ibn Sina. In this case, it causes confusion for researchers in the field of Islamic psychology.

3.3.5 Translation Challenges

As a result of conceptual confusion, there are difficulties in how to translate the concepts of Islamic psychology. For example, while there are those who translate the concept of nafs as 'self' in Islamic sources (Abu Raiya 2014), there are also those who translate it as 'soul' (Rothman and Coyle 2018). It is also equated with heart, intellect, or mind (Reza 2010). However, these English concepts are different from each other. This challenge is also present for the concepts of nonbelief such as *kafir* (nonbeliever), *mushrik* (idolater), and *muhafiq* (hypocrite) (Sevinç, Coleman, and Hood 2018). Moreover, translation difficulties in the field of Islamic psychology are not limited to English translation. Since Islam is a religion that has spread across a very wide geography and different cultures, both Islamic and psychology resources are full of examples of concepts and translations in different languages, as well as the diversity of Muslim countries. Although the first sources close to the Holy Quran and hadiths in these languages are mostly Arabic, there is rich Islamic literature in different languages over the centuries. For example, ruh, which is an Arabic concept, is also used as *ruh* in Turkish. *Ruh*, on the other hand, is translated as "soul," "spirit," as well as "psyche" in English. In Arabic, ruh mainly refers to soul and spirit, while nafs refers to psyche, therefore psychology is translated as 'ilm un nafs (psyche-logos) not 'ilm ur-ruh (soul/spirit-logos). However, in Turkish literature there is no such distinction and ruh is used for all. Moreover, the translation challenges of nouns make it difficult to translate their adjective forms as well. In Turkish, the terms psychological, spiritual, and mental are translated into the same word, *ruhsal*. Therefore, it becomes difficult to explain the differences between psychological, spiritual, and mental well-being, for example (Düzgüner 2021).

3.3.6 Measurement Challenges

Another consequence of the concept and translation confusion is the difficulty of definition and measurement. As a matter of fact, it is of great importance that the questions are correctly understood by the sample in scale development and scale adaptation studies. In Islamic psychology, the measurement difficulty is experienced in two ways. The first of these is the difficulties arising from the different understanding in an Islamic-based culture of the items of a scale developed in the West. Second, the lack of clarity in Islamic psychology concepts makes it difficult to develop scales as well as scale adaptation (Ağılkaya-Şahin 2015; Hökelekli 2016).

3.3.7 Practice Challenges

A similar situation to the measurement difficulty arises during the psychological practice phase. The psychotherapy and counseling techniques and treatment methods developed in the West may not fit the Muslim culture. For example, the frequent averting of a client's eyes during therapy is considered a clue that she/he is nervous or that she/he is lying. However, in Muslim cultures, men and women, especially those who are not related by blood, do not look directly into each other's eyes for a long time, occasionally averting their eyes for a few seconds during a conversation as a custom. Therefore, when working with a Muslim client, it is necessary to be aware of the effects of her/his faith on her/him in order to understand her/him correctly. Fortunately, the number of publications that underline this need and present an Islamic view in counseling and psychotherapy has increased (Abu Raiya and Pargament 2010; Ahmed and Amer 2012; Keshavarzi et al. 2021).

Although there are difficulties in studying Islam and psychology together, Islamic psychology studies are increasing day by day and continue to contribute to the psychology literature. Studies in this field not only shed light on the minds of Muslims but also offer an explanation of the human in general. In order to understand this unique approach correctly, it is necessary to know both Western and Islamic psychology literature well.

3.4 The Combination of Western and Islamic Psychologies

The common determination, which has been accepted throughout history, is that the human has a visible and an invisible side. Culture, religion, and personal perceptions are interrelated, and Islamic cultural heritage contains a human being model of this invisible side. On the other hand, psychology consists of different theories on this side of the human. Both of them share the same ground, the human being, but they split the psychological dimension of human into different pieces. Islamic sources use the terms such as nafs, qalb, ruh, and 'aql, while psychology uses the terms id-ego-superego, cognition, unconscious, self-actualization, and so on. Studies about Islam and psychology may include these terms in the same book. However, the term qalb may be confusing to a reader who is unfamiliar with Islamic literature. Likewise, explaining human behavior solely with a social conditioning process may be regarded as opposed to the Islamic understanding of free will and personal responsibility. So, Islamic psychology studies should be sensitive to its concepts. The title of the field, Islamic psychology, points at a combination of an Islamic and psychological understanding of the human. First of all, researchers have to make clear definitions and explanations of the basic terms and then they can share their Islamic psychology study.

To clarify how to combine Islamic and Western psychological understandings of human, we would like to present two diagrams (Figures 3 and 4). The rectangle symbolizes the invisible side of the human being, which is the same in both diagrams. The first (Figure 3) is the human in Islamic tradition and the second (Figure 4) is human in Western psychology. Islamic literature splits the rectangle into pieces such as nafs, ruh, qalb, 'aql and so on, while explaining her/his attitudes, behaviors, thoughts, attitudes and personality, etc. while Western psychology splits the rectangle into different types of pieces such as id-ego-superego, cognition, mind and so on. Since the human being is the same, Islamic and Western understandings also share common points somewhat.

Let us give an example to clarify the issue. *Nafs al-ammarah* in Islam and id in psychoanalysis are parts of the human. Nafs al-ammarah points at the stage whose main instinct is search of desire/lust (*shahwa*) and wrath (*gadhab*) for satisfaction. The term 'ammarah' means "the one who commands."

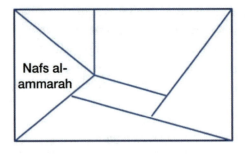

FIGURE 3
Human in Islamic literature

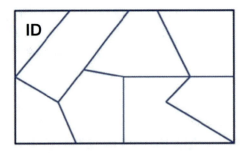

FIGURE 4
Human in Western psychology

So, nafs al-ammarah points at a selfish instinctive commander. It is also one of the essential parts of human existence in order to survive. Nafs al-ammarah in Islamic psychology is mostly likened to the id of Freud's theory because the id is defined as the primitive component of personality including the eros (libido) and the aggressive (death) instincts. Providing life energy, it is also a necessity to survive. At first glance, both seem the same. However, a researcher makes a big mistake if she/he claims that there is a triangle in both rectangles and therefore these triangles are the same. She/he should keep in mind that the triangles are different in position and size. In Islamic psychology, nafs is a concept used for the integrity of the human being and it is transformable from commanding to inspiring. Although it does not disappear completely, the intensity and power of the desires of nafs al-ammarah decreases as the level of nafs rises. In order to live happily in this world and hereafter these desires must be met to some extent, which points at the Islamic border between *halal* (acceptable) and *haram* (unacceptable). In psychoanalysis, the id is an unchangeable structure. It can be controlled by ego but there is no tendency to higher purposes in id-ego-superego theory. Moreover, this tendency depends on the pressure on the desires of id, namely the oedipal complex. So, there is a difference between the suppressed id and weakened nafs al-ammarah. The id is essential, while nafs al-ammarah is a means to reach higher levels of consciousness.

We have developed the above diagram because the topics that are in the scope of psychology today are frequently discussed in Islamic literature.

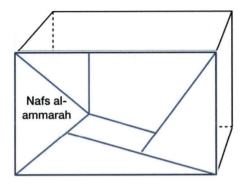

FIGURE 5
Nafs in Islamic literature

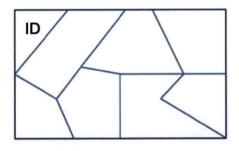

FIGURE 6
Psyche in Western psychology

Therefore, we would like to explain that both of them discuss their psychological aspects, such as perception, attitude, and personality, with their own systems and concepts. However, we need to emphasize here, that when we take a holistic approach to the Western psychological approach to the human and the Islamic view of the human, we actually get diagrams like those in Figures 5 and 6.

Unlike in the Western psychological approach, the human model of Islam is three-dimensional, not two. This three-dimensional model encompasses and transcends the other two dimensions. Therefore, there are psychological facts in Islamic literature, but these facts also have a third dimension. This third dimension consists of basic Islamic principles, such as that Allah (JJH) exists, that human and the universe are created by Him, that He is in contact with the human at all times, and that He offers the human a guide for life. According to Islam, everything in the universe has a spiritual background as well as physical functioning. For example, many verses in the Holy Quran provide explanations that are the same as today's astronomical, botanical, and geographical information: the earth and planets rotate in their orbits; plants, and trees grow, dry up, and turn green again; and sea waters do not mix with each other. The following verses shed light on these:

Neither can the sun overtake the moon, nor the night outpaces the day: Each of them keeps coursing in its orbit. (36/40)

It is He who sends down water from the skies and brings out of it everything that grows, the green foliage, the grain lying close, the date palm trees with clusters of dates, and the gardens of grapes, and of olives and pomegranates, so similar yet so unlike. Look at the fruits, how they appear on the trees, and they ripen. In all these are signs for those who believe. (6/99)

It is among His signs that the earth you see all barren and desolate begins to stir and sprout when We send down rain upon it. Surely, He who gives it life will also give life to the dead. (41/39)

It is He who made two bodies of water (in a sea) flow side by side, one fresh (and) sweet, the other brine (and) bitter, and has placed an interstice, a barrier between them. (25/53)

The Holy Quran also states that all living things on earth and in the sky remember Allah (JJH), adding a spiritual explanation to these scientific facts. The Holy Quran speaks of nature as Allah's (JJH) verses, encourages research on nature, and says that this research will result in admiration for the system and balance created by Allah (JJH). Examples are as follows:

The seven heavens and the earth and all that is therein, glorify Him and there is not a thing but glorifies His Praise. But you understand not their glorification. (17/44)

Do you see how all things in heavens and the earth, the sun, the moon, the stars, the mountains, trees and beasts, and men in abundance, pay homage to Allah (JJH)? (22/18)

So, in the Islamic perspective, the scientific explanation that "planets turn around the sun" and the spiritual explanation that "planets and sun pay homage to Allah (JJH)" do not contradict each other but coexist.

It is also possible to see the approach of adding a spiritual dimension to a known phenomenon in the hadiths of the Prophet Muhammad (PBUH). He accepted the known meanings of words and attributed a spiritual meaning to them, adding a third dimension to the concepts. For example, in this hadith, he gave a new meaning to the word 'the strong,' which means to be physically

VIEWS OF WESTERN AND ISLAMIC PSYCHOLOGY OF RELIGION

strong: *The strong is not the one who overcomes the people by his strength, but the strong is the one who controls himself while in anger* (Bukhari, Adab, 76). In another example, the prophet asked his companions, *Do you know who the bankrupt is?* The companions said, "A bankrupt is the one who has neither money nor wealth." The prophet said: *The bankrupt among my followers is he who would come on the Day of Judgment with prayers, fasting, and charity; but he had offended one person, slandered another, devoured others' wealth, shed the blood of this person, and beat that person. Each one of these people would be given some of the wrongdoer's good deeds. If his good deeds fall short of settling the account, then their sins will be taken from their accounts and thrown into his account, and he would be thrown in the Hellfire* (Muslim, Birr, 59).

This three-dimensional approach of Islam to life, in general, is also valid for explanations about the psychological aspect of human beings. For instance, psychological terms such as happiness, success, and love are used both for this world and hereafter. Actually, the human model in Islam begins before this world, continues in this world, and extends beyond; human came from Allah (JJH) and will return to Him (2/156). Therefore, all a person's attitudes and behaviors in this world are for the sake of Allah (JJH). Islam offers the human a guide for relationships with herself/himself, with their environment, and with their creator, Allah (JJH). The person is happy to the extent that she/he acts in accordance with this guide. For a Muslim, an attitude of believing in Allah (JJH) and directing her/his life as He wishes is the main element of her/his spiritual world. A person who believes in Allah (JJH) will evaluate all the events in this life in line with this belief, attach importance accordingly, and start a process of meaning-making in this direction. Therefore, in Islamic psychology, suggestions such as praying for a person who has psychological stress or reading the Holy Quran are frequently included, because in Islam, the psychological and spiritual aspects of the human are a whole. This spiritual aspect indicates that the front side of a phenomenon has a deeper background. So, we preferred to indicate this aspect as the third dimension in the diagram (Figure 5).

Western psychology considers the human in two dimensions since it excludes the existence of God and the norms based on it. However, in Islamic psychology, every psychological phenomenon has a spiritual meaning. Knowing this meaning is important for psychological study and practice. For example, a person diagnosed with obsessive-compulsive disorder (OCD) may develop a habit of constantly washing her/his hands. The psychiatrist may also apply the appropriate therapy technique to that person. However, a Muslim OCD client may also think that her/his ablution is not correct since she/he cannot be sure if her/his hands are clean. Ablution is an action of washing some parts of the body to begin *salah* (prayer) or to read the Holy Quran that provides spiritual purity. So, this client may feel spiritual stress added to the psychological one. In this case, OCD may not only be a psychological disorder that reduces the quality of life for that individual, but also a spiritual problem (see Erenay-Uyaver, Karatepe, and Tabo 2015). In order for the therapist to change this thought, she/he must also offer spiritual support or direct the client to a spiritual counselor. The concept of mental health in Islamic psychology also includes spiritual health.

Researchers should be sensitive while studying Western and Islamic psychologies together. They should keep in mind that although they have common points, Islamic psychology has a third dimension. Going back to the diagrams, Freud's id is a triangle, while nafs al-ammarah in Islam is a triangular prism. Islamic psychology professionals should know both Islam and psychology well. While studying both Western and Islamic psychologies, the true attitude is trying to understand both approaches in the wholeness of each, and then to determine the similarities and differences between them. This method consists of three levels: (1) comprehending the religious and cultural sources in the wholeness of them, (2) comprehending the psychological sources in the wholeness of them, and (3) determining the similarities and differences of both.

Religious and cultural heritage in general and Islamic literature in particular includes right determinations on the human being, besides psychology, consisting of useful techniques to overcome a problem. But their inner systems are different from each other. As researchers and psychologists, we should go to both sources to understand human nature and to better help clients from different religious and cultural backgrounds. Referring to these two sources is similar to modular arithmetic operations in mathematics. Currently, we use the mod 10 system, that is, the numbers between 0 and 9, but it is possible to operate in different modes such as mod 3, mod 5, or mod 9. Let us give an example with mod 5 and mod 10 (Figures 7–9). Here, mod 5 symbolizes the approach of Western psychology and mod 10 symbolizes the approach of Islamic psychology to the human. In this case, three possibilities arise.

In the first case (Figure 7), the operation with the same numbers in both systems gives the same results. These points are totally overlapping points of Western and Islamic psychologies. For example, in both approaches there is a visible aspect of human, namely her/his body, and an invisible aspect, that is, emotion, thought, attitude, personality, etc. Both explanations of the human accept that there is an interaction between the visible and invisible aspects of the human being. For example, psychological stress can cause headaches.

$$1\ 2\ 3\ \text{(mod 5)}$$
$$+\ 1\ 1\ 1\ \text{(mod 5)}$$
$$234\ \text{(mod 5)}$$

$$1\ 2\ 3\ \text{(mod 10)}$$
$$+\ 1\ 1\ 1\ \text{(mod 10)}$$
$$234\ \text{(mod 10)}$$

FIGURE 7 The first possibility of the determinations of Western and Islamic psychologies

$$1\ 2\ 3\ \text{(mod 5)}$$
$$2\ 3\ 4\ \text{(mod 5)}$$
$$+$$
$$412\ \text{(mod 5)}$$

$$1\ 2\ 3\ \text{(mod 10)}$$
$$2\ 3\ 4\ \text{(mod 10)}$$
$$+$$
$$357\ \text{(mod 10)}$$

FIGURE 8 The second possibility of the determinations of Western and Islamic psychologies

Naturally, both approaches suggest that these two aspects should be healed together in order to solve the problem permanently.

In the second case (Figure 8), the operation with the same numbers in both systems will not give the same results. This refers to situations where Western and Islamic psychologies have common elements, but their explanations for these elements are different. For example, happiness is a fundamental subject in Western and Islamic psychologies. Both approaches offer propositions about what happiness is and how to achieve it. While the definition of happiness and the ways to be happy in the first are limited to this life, in the second, happiness is considered as happiness in this world and the hereafter. Therefore, while the activities to be done to be happy include elements such as walking in nature and establishing healthy social relations, which are common in both, there are also elements such as reading the Holy Quran and praying for the happiness of the hereafter in Islamic psychology. Expressions such as "life satisfaction" may not have a very positive connotation for Muslims, since Islamic psychology does not see life as limited to this world. They have a life satisfaction that can be described as complacence of life or gladness of life.

In the third case (Figure 9), the numbers are processed in both systems and the results differ. This process also points to the functioning of elements in Islamic psychology that are not in Western psychology within its own system. For example, the qalb, one of the basic concepts of Islamic psychology, has no exact equivalent in modern psychology. However, Islamic psychology offers explanations about what qalb diseases are within its system and how to cure

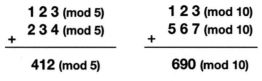

FIGURE 9   The third possibility of the determinations of Western and Islamic psychologies

them. Although there are some elements used by Western psychology in these explanations, the general approach and application are different. In Islamic psychology, disorders such as addiction, loss of anger control, and anxiety are among the diseases of the qalb as well as the moral elements such as arrogance, jealousy, and grudge.

The modular arithmetic example is actually valid for all characteristic systems seen in every approach to the human. The explanations and applications of the behavioral approach and those of the psychoanalytic approach are different. We cannot use the concept of *reinforcement* when describing Freud's views. This difference is not just a conceptual difference. These two approaches offer not only theory but also therapy techniques based on their theory. However, today we can benefit from both the behaviorist and the psychoanalytic approach at the same time. Islamic psychology is also an explanation of human beings and has a system within itself. The concepts in this system should be used appropriately and correctly. When we take a concept from Western psychology and use it in Islamic psychology without considering the general system of Islamic psychology, we make a mistake like using the concept of reinforcement when talking about Freud. On the other hand, when we see similar elements in Western psychology and Islamic psychology, we make a mistake when we say that they are the same without looking at their background. This is like arguing that Freud's individual subconscious and Jung's collective unconscious are the same, just because they both talk about unconscious processes. We cannot complete a picture with pieces of different puzzles, nor can we claim that these pieces are the same because they are the same color. The next chapter presents an attempt to explain how to use our model utilizing both approaches. This is not a comparison but a complementary view of Western and Islamic psychologies.

4   Complementary Views of Western and Islamic Psychologies

After Western psychology was established, different approaches to the human emerged, and over time these approaches gave birth to schools. Behaviorism, psychoanalysis, and humanistic psychology are accepted as the three most

VIEWS OF WESTERN AND ISLAMIC PSYCHOLOGY OF RELIGION

effective schools whose ways of explaining people are different from each other (Schultz and Schultz 2002). On the other hand, Islamic literature has a human model based on the Holy Quran and hadith. For centuries, Muslim scholars have discussed this human model with many methods, such as reasoning, introspection, observation, experiment, and experimentation. These studies also include the subjects that are in the field of modern psychology. Today, Islamic psychology adopts an intratextual model (Hood, Hill, and Williamson 2005) depending on the Holy Quran. The human model of Islamic psychology and the human theories of Western psychology contain similar and different points. These two approaches have the potential to contribute to each other. For this, it is necessary to know both areas well in their own integrity.

4.1 Complementary Views on the Islamic Model of the Human

Islamic psychology deals with the factors that affect people's feelings, thoughts, and behaviors. The basic concepts and their interaction with each other in the Islamic model of the human can be summarized as follows.

4.1.1 Ruh

According to Islam, the existence of the human starts before this world because Allah (JJH) created all ruhs first. In the Holy Quran, Allah (JJH) explains the scenery as He gathered all ruhs and then: *Allah asked, "Am I not your Lord?" They replied, "Yes, You are! We testify"* (7/172). Therefore, all ruhs have the experience of being in direct contact with Allah (JJH). Then ruhs come to this world one by one as a newly born baby. The verse *Surely We created you, then shaped you* (7/11) explains that the existence of the human goes back to her/his form body. When the ruh blows into a body a human being starts to live. This is the first moment of being a living organism. Allah (JJH) explains the creation of the human as *Then He made him complete and breathed into him of His ruh and made for you the ears and the eyes and the hearts; little is it that you give thanks* (32/9). So, the human being consists of a body and a ruh that knows the experience of being in contact with Allah (JJH). Even if the body and mind cannot remember that experience the ruh remembers and the nafs feels it. That is why the human has a natural tendency to feel the existence of a transcendent being. The body is temporal while the soul is infinite. At the moment of death the soul will leave the body and will continue to exist hereafter.

The Prophet Muhammad (PBUH) was asked about the nature of ruh frequently. Then Allah (JJH) revealed the verse: *They ask you O Prophet about the ruh. Say, "Its nature is known only to my Lord, and you O humanity have been given but little knowledge"* (17/85). Based on this verse, Muslim scholars preferred mainly to focus on the functions of ruh instead of its nature.

As explained in the first chapter, Western psychology became a scientific discipline at the end of a period of denying the existence of soul/spirit as well as other unseen deities. Psychological research focused on mind and mental processes instead. Since non-Western countries did not have such a background of change, they maintained the idea of body and soul/spirit about the existence of the human. That is why the term psychology is translated as the science of soul/spirit. Even today, 'mental health' is termed as *ruh sağlığı*, which means "health of soul/spirit" in Turkish, although the psychologists insisted on the idea that psychology never investigates the soul. Psychologists and psychiatrists still use this term for mental health and *ruh hastalığı* (disease of soul/spirit) for psychological disorders. The reason behind Turkish psychologists' insistence on the term ruh depends on religious and cultural understanding that the human consists of body and soul/spirit. Even if they accept that psychological phenomena stem from biochemical processes, not an unseen being, they continue to use the term ruh. However, in Islamic psychology, ruh is the essence that blows into the human body and makes it alive. Actually, ruh is an essence and it is qalb that becomes ill. Although the functions of ruh, such as thinking, reasoning, and remembering, take part in modern psychology, the essence of ruh in Islamic psychology has no place in modern psychology.

4.1.2   Nafs

Islamic sources mainly use the term nafs when discussing human. In short, nafs is used to describe the human being in the psychosomatic integrity of the soul/spirit and body in Islamic psychology. In other words, when ruh enters the body it becomes alive and this whole existence is called nafs. There are many verses in the Holy Quran about nafs, with different meanings. The first meaning is the species of human, namely humankind (9/128). The second one is the person herself/himself (6/152; 4/29, 113). In some verses, Allah (JJH) uses the term to point at the heart or inner world (3/154; 4/63), and the center of desires (12/53; 21/102).

The features of nafs reflect the understanding of the human in Islam and is essential in Islamic psychology. Depending on ruh, nafs has a natural tendency to higher purposes and to transcendence, while it has a natural tendency to reach worldly desires and to be selfish, depending on the body. Nafs can choose to do good or evil with its free will. Ibn Rushd (2007: 10) defined the nafs as the principle that provides the unity and integrity of the body, and accordingly it cannot be deprived of the body. In this case, the nafs is the aspect that enables the existence and survival of people in this world, but it also includes the part that directs people to extremism. Therefore, it is not possible to completely dismantle and dispose of this side of the human, but it is possible to train it to reach higher levels of consciousness (Hujwiri 2014: 269). So, nafs can be and ought to be controlled and thus it can be purified and developed. It is the place where experiences from the soul and the body are experienced. Since a physical change like pain and a psychospiritual change like sorrow are experienced by the nafs, it covers the entire inner world of the human being.

The term nafs has several translations in English: "self," "I," "personality," and "desire." Also, the term psyche is similar to nafs. The meaning of psyche is "soul," "personality," and "the totality of elements forming the mind." In English, "psyche often sounds less spiritual than soul, less intellectual than mind, and more private than personality" (Merriam-Webster 2021). In the *APA Dictionary of Psychology*, psyche is defined as "the mind in its totality, as distinguished from the physical organism" (Vandenbos 2015: 852). They are similar to each other on the point that both nafs and psyche are used as a general term for the unseen part of human existence. The Arabic translation of psychology is 'ilm un-nafs that consists of 'logos' and 'nafs' as psychology consists of 'psyche' and 'logos.' However, the approaches to psyche and nafs are different. Western psychology regards the psyche as a structure or a flow, to discover how it works and functions from a descriptive point of view, while Islamic psychology regards nafs as a dynamic essence that can be purified and developed due to the normative approach.

4.1.3 Qalb

The center of nafs is the qalb in Islamic psychology. The lexical meaning of the qalb is heart, but terminological meanings of both differ. The term heart refers to both an organ in the body and the center of emotions in general. For instance, one draws a shape of heart to express love as seen in the graffiti "I love you." The heart is used to express excitement such as in the sentences that "my heart was beating out of my chest." Also "broken heart" points to unhappiness and disappointment. Moreover, the heart has a cognitive usage to some degree in English as well. For instance, "to know something by heart" means "to memorize/to know the issue very well," which points at the memory, not emotions. Although the term heart is used with these meanings in daily language, its usage in Western psychological literature is very rare. When searching for 'heart' in psychology literature, one will encounter the term 'cardiac psychology,' which is defined as "an emerging subspeciality of behavioral medicine that studies how behavioral, emotional, and oscial factors influence the development, progression, and treatment of coronary heart disease (CHD)" (Vandenbos 2015: 157). Although the heart has cognitive and emotional meanings in daily language, Western psychology regards the heart as an organ in the body instead of a psychological element like cognition, memory, or mind.

The term heart is difficult to translate in non-Western cultures, as the meanings of heart in English and in the psychology literature are different. For instance, heart is *kokoro* in Japanese. Additional to the emotional connotations, kokoro is written on the small pools in the gardens of temples and shrines. Shinto-Buddhists wash their hands and face for spiritual cleansing before the entrance. A Japanese statement is written with a meaning of "heart purifying point," on these pools pointing at a spiritual heart. Toshihiko and Toyo Izutsu preferred to translate the term kokoro as 'mind' in their book with this explanation:

> The way Tsurayuki mentions the kokoro (mind) suggests that it is not to be understood as a particular state of subjectivity or of the consciousness which has already been activated toward artistic creativity. Rather, it is structurally posited by Tsurayuki as the ground not merely of poetic creation but of all psychological and cognitive activities or experiences of the subject. The implication of this is that the kokoro is supposed to be a sort of psychic potentiality or dynamics of the subject to be activated – when stirred and stimulated by the external things and events – into function, manifesting itself as omoi (thought, thinking, including images and ideas) and jō (feeling emotion).
>
> TOSHIHIKO AND TOYO IZUTSU 1981: 7

Interestingly, the usage of kokoro in Japanese is so similar to the usage of qalb in Islamic psychology. The qalb is a psychological ground where internal and external forces leave a mark. The qalb has been explained with the analogy of a pool with various channels. The information gained via five senses flows into the qalb from one channel and the experiences learned via training flow from another. Also, desires such as aggression and passion and imaginings such as dreaming flow from other channels. The information and experiences gained via the five senses are external channels while imagination, wrath, or lust resulting from the person's temperament are internal channels. These many channels always flow into the qalb, which means it is always in the state of flux. So, all thoughts, feelings, experiences, information, and images have an effect on the qalb (Ghazali 1992, v. 4: 10).

Qalb in Islamic psychology is similar but not limited to the term mind in Western psychology. We can briefly explain the qalb as the cognitive and emotional center of the psychological and spiritual existence of the human. In other words, the organ heart is the center of the body and the spiritual heart is the center of nafs; the human behaves in parallel with her/his qalb. In the Holy Quran, the term qalb is mentioned 132 times with features such as "that finds

VIEWS OF WESTERN AND ISLAMIC PSYCHOLOGY OF RELIGION

the true way," "that gets ill" and "that is celebrated by" (Yılmaz 2020). The verses about qalb shed light on the subject:

> Those who have no knowledge say, "If only Allah (JJH) would speak to us or a sign would come to us!" The same was said by those who came before. Their hearts are all alike. (2/118)

> Allah (JJH) will not hold you accountable for unintentional oaths, but for what you intended in your hearts. (2/225)

> Why did they not humble themselves when We made them suffer? Instead, their hearts were hardened. (6/43)

> They have hearts they do not understand with, eyes they do not see with, and ears they do not hear with. (7/179)

As seen, the qalb is the center for intentions, thoughts, and making decisions; it is the psychospiritual element the person understands with. In this case, the qalb is similar to the term mind in Western psychology. The statement "hardened-heart" is mentioned many times in the Holy Quran with the meaning of being close-minded. Those who never change their point of view and ideas and those who insist on their customs without any logical explanation are being criticized as having a heart like a stone. Moreover, the qalb is not only the center for thoughts but also emotions, as in these verses:

> No one would ask for exemption except those who have no faith in Allah (JJH) or the Last Day, and whose hearts are in doubt. (9/45)

> Indeed, there is more fear in their hearts for you believers than for Allah (JJH). That is because they are people who do not comprehend. (59/13)

> Those who believe and whose hearts find comfort in the remembrance of Allah (JJH). Surely in the remembrance of Allah (JJH) do hearts find comfort/peace. (13/28)

Feelings such as doubt, fear, and peace occur in the qalb. When the qalb is full of doubt or fear the individual behaves in that way. When the qalb is full of peace the person experiences tranquility. Remembrance of Allah (JJH) is the best way to get peace of mind (13/28), in other words, the heart's ease in Islamic psychology.

The notion of a psychospiritual center where all inner and outer effects on cognition and emotion occur may be useful in Western psychology. The recently popularized idea of mindfulness similarly refers to such a unity that insists on awareness, feeling, and peace that goes beyond the mind. Qalb, a broader concept than mind, also points to the center of the whole psyche.

4.1.4 'Aql

In Islam, the human is responsible for her/his actions because she/he has the free will that means having the right to choose. The thinking and decision-making psychospiritual element of the human is 'aql.

According to the Holy Quran, it is 'aql that distinguishes the human from other beings, providing meaning-making to all her/his actions and enabling her/him to take responsibility before Allah (JJH). The term and its variations are mentioned in forty-nine verses in the Holy Quran with the meaning of reasonable thinking and correct inference as follows:

> These are precepts of wisdom We offer to men, but only those who are rational understand. (29/43)

> They are deaf, dumb and blind, and they fail to understand (they do not use their reason). (2/171)

> This is how Allah (JJH) explains His verses to you so that you may understand (think about these). (2/242)

In these verses, the importance of 'reasoning,' that is, thinking correctly by using the mind, is emphasized. In the Quranic terminology, 'aql is described as "a power to acquire knowledge" and "knowledge obtained through this power." The knowledge gained through the mind must be used under the control of this power, 'aql. 'Aql seems similar to reason and intellect. Western psychology prefers cognition instead. The reasoning sounds normative since it is an ability to separate true and false while cognition sounds descriptive since it means knowing something as it is. Actually, 'aql refers to cognition that works properly in a sense. So cognitive disorders are like a situation where 'aql cannot deduce rightly. Mental and cognitive disorders were identified as 'aql disorders (*akıl hastalıkları*) in some Muslim countries because 'aql is the center for reasoning and decision-making.

Many emotions and thoughts gather in the qalb from various channels. 'Aql considers all of these, makes a decision, and chooses the behavior. There are two basic sources to guide 'aql in its decision about what is right and what is

VIEWS OF WESTERN AND ISLAMIC PSYCHOLOGY OF RELIGION 61

wrong. The first is an external source consisting of the knowledge from the Holy Quran and hadith and the second is an internal source called *fitrah*.

4.1.5   Fitrah

With a lexical meaning of "the first state of creation, clean and original nature," fitrah is a term that expresses the initial pure and essential state of the human being that emerged as a result of Allah's (JJH) act of creation. In the Holy Quran and hadiths of the Prophet Muhammad (PBUH), fitrah is used to denote the essence of the human personality that exists independently of the environmental effects and the development capacity that is common for all people. Fitrah is a natural tendency to the good, the right, and the beautiful. Also, there is a tendency to recognize the existence and oneness of God. Muslim scholars generally admit that this tendency is related to the contract made between the ruhs of humans and Allah (JJH) at the time of the first creation as mentioned above. Allah (JJH) explains the nature of fitrah in the Holy Quran as: *So, direct your face [i.e., self] toward the religion, inclining to truth. [Adhere to] the fitrah of Allah (JJH) upon which He has created [all] people. No change should there be in the creation of Allah (JJH). That is the correct religion, but most of the people do not know* (30/30).

It is worth noting that the term fitrah brings to mind two figures in modern psychology: Jung and Maslow. Since the concept of the collective unconscious of Jung's theory refers to a common area of all human beings it resembles fitrah in Islamic psychology. Jung traveled to experience many cultures and investigated various mystical teachings. He realized a common essence of all human beings and called it the collective unconscious. He claimed that it is not possible to know the collective unconscious by the intellect but through intuition (Jung 2008: 71). The features of the collective unconscious are similar to fitrah, however, fitrah is not a common structure consisting of various components as collective unconscious that consists of archetypes. It is rather a tendency toward the good, the right, the beautiful, and toward Allah (JJH) at last. That's why fitrah is seen as the basis of morality while there is no direct relation between collective unconscious and morality.

Maslow (2001: 8–9) argued that each individual has an invariable inner nature. This nature can be influenced by habits, cultural pressure, and negative attitudes. If this structure is rejected or suppressed, human health worsens. Also, the human has a natural tendency toward self-actualization. This tendency and fitrah are similar to each other. However, Maslow's inner nature is a structure that takes shape according to the culture, that is, although it is the same for everyone at first, it changes over time according to the conditions in which the person lives. However, human nature in Islam does not change.

In addition, according to Maslow, this inner nature is neutral, while according to Islam, the human has a good essence. Depending on the circumstances, the qalb and 'aql may start to work incorrectly and make incorrect inferences. In the end, the person may commit wrongful acts contrary to the pure essence of human nature. However, with regret and repentance, she/he can leave this mistake and clean her/his qalb and start to act in accordance with her/his pure nature (fitrah) again.

4.1.6 Interaction among Basic Concepts of Islamic Psychology

The body of the human is mortal while their ruh is eternal and they are linked to this world with their body and linked to the other world with their ruh. The qalb, the psychospiritual center of the human, makes efforts to get a balance between nafs and ruh. While ruh has the knowledge of higher purposes, nafs tends to worldly desires because of its bodily desires. Therefore, nafs should be controlled and disciplined. By purifying the nafs, the human may transform from mortal being to human being and mature human. In other words, the process of purifying the nafs is a psychospiritual development that starts with a mortal being and continues with being human. At the upper levels of purification few humans may become a mature human (*insan-i kamil*).

Hujwiri (2014: 262), a great Sufi of the eleventh century, explained the forces that competed in the human as a tension between the nafs and the ruh. According to him, the nafs of the human tries to drag her/him to hell while the ruh invites them to heaven. Opposing the worldly desires of nafs will strengthen 'aql. The qalb is not only the center of emotions but a center of understanding, and the ruh is like a door to the higher worlds. The qalb is a space for ingenuity that includes deep intelligence and lore. The goal of the human is to have a compassionate qalb and to improve its understanding. The nafs, which has various levels, contains all negative emotions at the lowest level. However, the nafs can be purified and enlightened gradually (Frager 2005: 28; Kayıklık 2011a: 85; Karaca 2011: 204; Yüksel and Karacoşkun 2013: 236). As long as the qalb is under the influence of the nafs, full of worldly desires the person cannot progress on the path of spiritual development and becomes more mortal. Nut as long as the qalb abodes by the ruh that calls to higher purposes, the person becomes more human (Figure 10).

It is also important to discuss that two different human forces competing with each other are seen throughout history from philosophical schools to mystical traditions. Freud's theory of personality based on the ego between id and superego is one of them. In Islamic psychology, on the other hand, there is a model built on the heart between the nafs and the soul. Even if these models are based on dual contention, it is difficult to say that these models overlap.

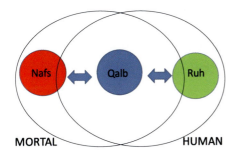

FIGURE 10
Human and mortal in the trilogy of qalb, nafs, and ruh
SOURCE: AYTEN AND DÜZGÜNER 2017: 52

Indeed, in Freud's theory, the ego has to choose between the need for instinctual satisfaction from the id and the moral and social norms from the superego. In Islamic psychology, the qalb tries to balance between the misty desires coming from the nafs and divine inspiration from the soul. Inspiration from Allah (JJH) or any spiritual transcendent is out of the question for Freud. According to him, experiencing such a religious or mystical experience is nothing more than some kind of obsession and subconscious feelings of guilt and helplessness (Freud 2006a, 2006b, 2006c). Although competing components seem similar, they are different in their background. Rothman and Coyle (2018) present a successful figure to explain the Islamic human model.

The mirror metaphor is frequently used in Islamic literature, which is helpful in making the human model of Islam clearer. The human qalb is like a clean mirror; its nature, namely fitrah, is providing a bright image. When the manifestation of Allah (JJH) is reflected in this qalb, the truth is seen clearly and distinctly. However, the qalb, which is pure from birth, is rusted by the judgments of the environment in which a person was born, by what she/he learned from their surroundings, by the mistakes made, and by their bad thoughts and behaviors. The rusty mirror does not reflect the truth, namely light, as it is. In other words, the person cannot think and decide correctly, she/he cannot see the evil in mistakes, and cannot feel peaceful. This qalb cannot fully fulfill its function and so becomes sick. In Islamic psychology, diseases of qalb mean its contamination and loss of function. It is possible to clean the qalb and regain its health with various methods and applications. However, if a person does not clean the rust from her/his qalb, over time it will cover the whole qalb and it will no longer work as it is in its nature. In that case, the qalb loses the ability to think correctly and feel good. This is called the hardening of the heart. People with such hardened hearts become closed-minded and fail to see the truth. The Prophet Muhammad (PBUH) explains this process as: *Verily when a person commits a sin, a black mark appears upon his heart. If he abandons the sin, seeks forgiveness, and repents, then his heart will be polished. If he returns to the sin, the blackness will be increased until it overcomes his heart* (Thirmizi, Tafsiru ul-Quran, 83). Also, a relevant verse in the Holy Quran says: *When Our revelations are recited before him, he says: "These are fables of long ago. No. In fact what they have been doing has rusted their hearts"* (83/13–14). These rusty and hardened qalbs cannot feel peace either.

One of the main purposes in Islam is to ensure the happiness of the person in this world and hereafter. For this, the person needs to get rid of qalb diseases and clean her/his qalb. But the human is not a perfect being, often making mistakes. In such cases, she/he should immediately repent and try to clear her/his heart by compensating for their mistake. Purification of the qalb means that the nafs reduces worldly desires and turns to higher goals. In Islam, there are various techniques and practices, especially worships, for cleansing the qalb and raising the nafs to higher levels. As the level of the nafs rises, the person's view also changes, and her/his consciousness rises as well. Her/his attributions to the events, their coping capacity with difficulties, and attitudes toward others and incidents also change.

This point of view is common in Islamic disciplines, which developed over time and determined their own limits. *Tafsir* focuses on the interpretation of verses and hadith focuses on the source and explanation of hadith and sunnah, and words and deeds of the Prophet Muhammad (PBUH). Those who write tafsir are called *mufassir*, and those who study hadith are called *muhaddith*. *Fiqh*, on the other hand, specializes in making judgments from basic sources. Those who practice fiqh are called *faqih*. Over time, Islam spread to different lands and Muslims encountered different cultures. Muslims who encountered different theologies also developed Islamic theology under the name of *kalam*. Those who produced works on these subjects were theologians. Tasawwuf, one of the Islamic disciplines, is actually based on the application of the Holy Quran and the Sunnah in daily life. It focuses on getting to the upper consciousness levels by taking the human nafs under control. People who engage in this personal purification process are also called Sufis. Therefore, in the history of Islam, a person can be both a Sufi and a theologian. In other words, Sufis are not a separate class, but people who try to develop their own nafs under the conditions they are in, and who not only perform their prayers as a mission but also try to feel awe. Therefore, the essence of Tasawwuf is to implement Islam. Since the essence of Islam is the human's turning to Allah (JJH), Tasawwuf has been a field that contains many explanations about the human and plenty of practices in various Sufi groups (Düzgüner 2007; Gürses 2019). For this reason, Sufi studies frequently refer to the subjects of Islamic psychology because Tasawwuf offers a systematic psychospiritual development model.

4.2 Complementary Views on the Psychospiritual Development of Human

Tasawwuf is a way of spiritual and moral cleansing. In this way, people try to go toward Allah (JJH) by moving from their own self (Topçu 2005; 134). According to Arasteh and Sheikh (2010: 62), Tasawwuf is an individuation process. This process consists of extinction (*fanā'*) and existence (*bakā'*). Fanā' is the process of getting rid of the negative orientations of the individual, while bakā' is a process that involves the virtues and integration with the upper self, trying to acquire morality and thus trying to reach one's own integrity. It is also possible to come across examples of personal development in Western psychology and the transformation of nafs Tasawwuf. Jung's individuation process, Maslow's development stages, and transpersonal psychologists' consciousness spectrum theories are among these. While examining the handling of personality transformation in both Tasawwuf and psychology, it is necessary to identify similar and different points, otherwise there may be the risk of misconception. In this section, the transformation of the nafs will be handled in terms of Islamic Tasawwuf and Western psychology trying to be careful on sensitive points of studying in two areas.

In Tasawwuf, the first thing to keep in mind for a person who has taken the road of spiritual transformation is that she/he is a person who is being trained (*mureed/derwish*). This training process causes the person to turn her/his attention to her/himself and to be subjected to the questions of "who am I, why do I exist, where do I come from and where do I go to?" She/he realizes that Allah (JJH) does not create them and the universe in vain and does not leave it alone (75/36; 38/27, 3/191). Then she/he understands that she/he was sent to this world to be tested by choosing the good or bad. The retribution of this choice is eternal blessing or eternal torment in the hereafter (Muhasibi 1998: 199). The spiritual journey has several stages. These were four degrees in the beginning, then three degrees were added to this model (Küçük 2011: 62). We can summarize these stages, which indicate different states of nafs as follows (see Ayten and Düzgüner 2017).

4.2.1 *Nafs al-ammarah* (The Commanding Nafs)

It is the lowest rebellious nafs that drives people away from Allah (JJH). *Ammarah* means very commanding, and is named because of the Surah Yusuf, the fifty-third verse: *Except for what my Lord has captured, he will certainly order evil* (12/53). The nafs is born to this world and finds herself/himself with a sensual life, habits, and tastes. In this state, the pursuit of satisfaction of desire (lust) and anger is the main driver of all behaviors. Therefore, there is no serious will to comply with religious and moral rules. People may begin to commit sins deliberately, forgetting to repent. Since the idea of repentance (*tawbah*) does not come to their mind, they do not feel sorry for their mistake and insist on sins (Ghazali 1992, v. 4: 83). The nafs at this stage is like a mirror that is completely rusted and reflects nothing.

The Sufis have admitted that the nafs at the stage of commanding is the center where evil and ugly deeds arose. There are two types of rust: sins that are the result of the human's mistakes, and bad emotions and habits, such as arrogance, envy, and stinginess. However, it is possible to get rid of both types (Hujwiri 2014: 259–260). When the Sufis use the term nafs alone they mean this type of nafs. For example, when they talk about moving away from the desires and aspirations of the nafs, it is meant to move away from the desires of the nafs al-ammarah that command evil.

Descriptions of Tasawwuf about this type of nafs evoke the concept of the id in Freud's personality theory. Indeed, according to Freud, personality consists of three basic structures, the id, ego, and superego. The id contains all innate biological impulses. Working with the principle of pleasure, it puts pressure on the ego to fulfill its wishes immediately. The main ruling forces of the id are sexuality and aggression. On the other hand, the superego, which includes social rules and moral laws, pressures the ego to restrict itself. Trying to balance between id and superego, the ego acts within the framework of reason, logic, and consciousness. The ego takes the needed energy from the id, which is the energy source of life. Occasionally, the ego lets its wishes fulfill the needs that enable human to survive. It also tries to establish a balance by following the superego's instructions in order to fulfill goals such as self-protection and public acceptance. The personality of the human is shaped according to which of these elements are dominant (Freud 2004).

It can be said that the concept of the nafs al-ammarah in Tasawwuf and the id concept of Freud have similarities in various aspects. Both symbolize the selfish side of the human. This is the source of all kinds of material pleasures and ambitions, from dignity to food. Aggression and sexuality are the main elements in both. In addition, the id is necessary for the principle of sustaining life, the most basic impulse of the human, and it is the source of life energy. According to Tasawwuf, although the dominant feature of this type of nafs is worldly desires, the nafs is a necessity to survive. Sufis generally use the metaphor of horse and rider to explain nafs and ruh. The nafs is like a horse of the ruh. If the human releases the reins and leaves her/himself in the direction it is going, she/he will be destroyed. If she/he tries to kill it, then she/he lost their vehicle on the path of truth. So, the rider should take control of the horse and keep going (Ghazali 1992; Rumi, v. 5, *c.*153).

VIEWS OF WESTERN AND ISLAMIC PSYCHOLOGY OF RELIGION 67

Looking at these similarities, one should not think that both concepts are the same. In Freud's theory, the id is a basic structure of the human, representing the natural possessive and destructive power that exists in every human being. However, in Tasawwuf, the dark side of the nafs is more like rust or a curtain than a constant structure. Tasawwuf is based on the principle that it is possible to purify the nafs by getting rid of these curtains or cleaning the rust. For example, Hujwiri (2014: 259–260) mentioned the two evil sides of the nafs: the mistakes and the bad habits. According to him, while it is possible to get rid of sins by *tawbah* (repentance), the way to break the bad habits is *riyazah* (abstemiousness). Sins are external, and bad natures are internal features. The lower internal features can be purified by the higher external qualities. The external bad features can also be cleaned with the internal good qualities.

4.2.2   *Nafs al-lawwamah* (The Accusing Nafs)

The first requirement to go to the next stage, *nafs al-lawwamah*, is the questioning of the person her/himself and accepting that she/he made a mistake. Nafs al-lawwamah is the nafs that makes effort to leave her/his negative attitudes and behaviors via self-questioning. The term *lawwamah* means the one who is very regretful. It was named as nafs al-lawwamah based on the second verse of Surah al-Qiyamah: *And I swear by the self-accusing nafs* (75/2). At this stage, the person is sometimes defeated by her/his desires, and sometimes exhibits behaviors that comply with moral values. The person intends to clean the rusted mirror. The nafs al-lawwamah involves both repentance to all sins in general and repentance at every single mistake and an effort to stand behind her/his repentance, namely trying not to make the same mistake again.

Nafs al-lawwamah is the first step of spiritual purification since the person decides to clean her/his qalb by opposing the commanding nafs (nafs al-ammarah) and decides to transform her/himself. According to Muhasibi (1998: 198–199), it is with a personal awareness that a person enters the path of spiritual purification. According to him, this first step is to review one's life and decide to organize it in the direction of Allah's (JJH) will. In this process, the person reviews how much she/he has done the things that Allah (JJH) warns people not to do and how much she/he has not done the things that Allah (JJH) wants people to fulfill. Even if the person regards her/himself as a Muslim and Sufi, they can be a sinful person. Therefore, one should first question oneself with sincerity and be ready to change in order to increase ones spiritual level in the sight of Allah (JJH).

Questioning oneself is reminiscent of the superego in Western psychology. Consisting of social norms and moral principles, the superego always says no to the desires of the id and judges the ego. People under the dominance of the superego are inclined to accuse themselves more, which may lead to personality disorders. Although the ego under the influence of the superego and nafs al-lawwamah are similar in respect of self-accusing, the reasons for judging are different. While the superego makes judgments depending on human-made norms and rules, nafs al-lawwamah question her/himself according to Allah's (JJH) will. Social norms and information thought by the surroundings may be rust on the qalb if these are not in accordance with Islam because the source of moral principles and religious rules is Allah (JJH).

On the other hand, there is an inner voice that whispers to be right and compassionate based on fitrah in Tasawwuf as well. The inner voice that invites the person to act correctly is often called conscience (*wijdan*). It is explained by the conscience of the person to be honest and compassionate to other living things. When people harm others by making mistakes, they suffer remorse, which stems from conscience. The conscience becomes stronger once the nafs reaches upper levels. Actually, it is possible to see the representation of the inner voice that says what to do in many movies, animations, and cartoons. When the character is about to harm an innocent figure, its miniature silhouettes appear on both sides of its head. The silhouette of the horned figure carrying a sickle in his hand whispers to harm, while his winged silhouette, which has a halo on his head, tells him to be compassionate. This voice that tells a person to act correctly is similar to conscience. Positive psychology refers to such an inner voice. According to this approach, the human is good by nature and tends to the good. Learning and conditioning processes are effective on the harmful and destructive actions of the human, and therefore, pure inner nature may not emerge due to the environment. In other words, the inner voice that tells people to behave virtually is based on the essence of being human (Zulliger 1998). This approach is similar to the Islamic view of conscience (wijdan) that is the inner voice from the pure nature of human (fitrah). Yet, there is also an outer voice in Tasawwuf which will be mentioned in the next section.

In Tasawwuf the relationship between the human and Allah (JJH) depends on love. Therefore, to do something that Allah (JJH) does not want means to go against the one you love. According to Ghazali (1992, v. 4: 9), repentance (tawbah) consists of "knowledge," "state of consciousness," and "action." Knowledge is to realize the harms of the mistake/sin and being away from Allah (JJH), her/his beloved one. When one is sure of being distant from the beloved one, Allah (JJH), she/he feels pain because of their fault. It is regret. When the heart is full of this pain, the person regrets and becomes motivated not to make the same mistake again. So, repentance is not just about regret but a complicated process including correcting the mistake in the past error, having willpower today, and deciding not to repeat it in the future. As seen, Tasawwuf discusses the emotional, operational, and motivational dimensions of regret and repentance.

Western psychology discusses similar issues as well. From a psychological perspective, regret is defined as "an emotional response to the remembrance of a past state, condition, or experience that one wishes had been different" (Vandenbos 2015: 896). Zeelenberg et al. (1996: 18) explain regret as "If a decision turns out badly, we often kick ourselves for not having done something different. This is especially true if we learn that the alternative course of action would have resulted in a more favorable outcome." There is a state of awareness about the past and the experience of negative emotion in regret. From daily routines to high-level cognitive inquiries, one can experience regrets anytime.

According to Zeelenberg (1999), in order for a person to feel regret, they must first go through a cognitive process in which they must think about their choices and consequences. There are two important actions here for regret. The first is thinking, evaluating the events or situations in one's mind, and making inferences, and the second is feeling the regret experienced when the event or situation causes pain to the person (Özdemir and Düzgüner 2020). Regret may also occur as a result of an action the person considers wrong as well as in situations when the person does not act, even though they feel like they should do something (Gilovich and Medvec 1995: 380). This regret mostly leans on the feeling of discomfort that comes from not fulfilling the responsibility.

Islamic psychology and Western psychology are in agreement that regret is not just an emotion, but a cognitive process that leads to behavior change. However, they differ in what is considered a mistake. In Western psychology, it is the person who decides the wrong behavior according to the consequences of the action. However, a mistake in Islamic psychology is an area where Allah (JJH) draws the boundaries as well as the person. In this area, a person has responsibilities toward her/himself, other living things, and Allah (JJH). The person may experience regret when they do not fulfill these responsibilities. Although there are differences about who will determine the area of responsibility, Islamic and Western psychology agree that one feels regret when one does not fulfill responsibilities. Here it should be noted that the responsibility area in Islam is not limited to organized worships such as five-times-a-day prayer (salah) or fasting during Ramadan. Responsibility includes having good relations, such as taking care of family members, caring about neighbors, visiting relatives, or even smiling and being kind to others. Responsibility also includes saving nature, feeding animals, and taking care of plants based on the idea that human beings borrowed nature from Allah (JJH), so care is required in relations with nature (see Ayten 2021). A Muslim feels regretful when they miss morning salah, as well as when they harm nature or break up family relations, which is committing a mistake against Allah's (JJH) will.

Feeling regretful is also mentioned in Western psychology literature. The effect of regret on the person occurs in two ways. In the first, one can experience the regret of constantly accusing her/himself, which then turns to chronic regret. This is a kind of obsessive thinking or cyclical obsession in psychology. In the second case, the person motivates her/himself not to repeat his mistake just after feeling regretful. In other words, the first reaction is coming full circle, while the second is more consciously moving forward. The psychology literature has addressed this situation with regret being divided into past and future regret. In past regret, the person carried out an action (or inaction) that they deemed wrong and has now experienced regret. In future-oriented regret, the person tends to determine her/his action accordingly by predicting that they may regret in the future before carrying out an action (Shani, Danziger, and Zeelenberg 2015).

The nafs al-lawwamah stage points to both past and future regret. As a matter of fact, Islamic literature does not interpret this level of nafs as being stuck in a person's mistake. Nafs al-lawwamah also includes a constructive process in the form of learning from the error and trying not to do it again. Islam and Tasawwuf warns people against being stuck in regret. For example, Rumi points to this fact in *Mathnawi*: *It is a mistake to pity the past. It has gone! There is no benefit to remember it* (v. 4, c.2024). He breaks the regret circle of thought saying: *Pull yourself together. Be careful from now on. Because the door of repentance is open with the permission of Allah* (JJH) (v. 4, c.2504). The expression of *nasuh repentance* mentioned in the Holy Quran (66/8) indicates that the person made a definite decision not to fall again in a situation. Therefore, regret in Sufi literature points to a process that extends to both the past and the future.

Moreover, Islamic psychology presents a dynamic description and a significant classification of regret. Hujwiri (2014: 357) states that the first station on the way to Allah (JJH) is repentance. The word tawbah means "return, go back, give up." It has three components. The first is the regret of being opposed to divine provisions. The second is to immediately abandon mistakes, defects, and sin. The third is to decide not to make the sin/mistake again. Moreover, Hujwiri asserts three types of repentance that direct the person to repent. The first type of regret (tawbah) depends on the fear of punishment. It is about obeying, or not, the rules. The second type of repentance (*anabah*) is caused by the awareness that divine blessings are better than the wealth of this world. It stems from a realization that being too busy with worldly issues is meaningless.

VIEWS OF WESTERN AND ISLAMIC PSYCHOLOGY OF RELIGION   71

When the person realizes that they are too busy with worldly affairs and that they do fewer acts that will be permanent in the hereafter – such as worshipping, helping others, giving charity – this type of repentance is experienced. This is not about committing a sin but an awareness to be careful about deeds. The third type of repentance (*awbah*) points at a higher level of awareness that Allah (JJH) witnesses all. This repentance stems from feeling shy in front of Allah (JJH). The reason behind repentance is different in these levels. After being regretful, the person decides to change her/his actions because of the fear of punishment at the first level, for the request of good deeds (*thawāb*) at the second level, and for the sake of Allah (JJH) only at the third level. So, Hujwiri pointed out that different repentance would emerge in different states of consciousness. This gradual classification is worthy of study from a psychological perspective. Types of regret that are differentiated as the level of consciousness in Islamic psychology is a unique point of view. Islam does not only provide a to-do or not-to-do list, but also emphasizes a direct relationship with Allah (JJH). The awareness that Allah (JJH) sees His servant at all times changes the person's feelings, thoughts, and behaviors as well as the type of regret. It is a deep spiritual experience to try to act correctly at every moment just for the sake of Allah (JJH), the beloved one.

4.2.3   *Nafs al-mulhimah* (The Inspired Nafs)

At this stage, the spiritual aspect of the nafs extends beyond itself by controlling the physical needs. This means the domination over the physical aspect of the self by its spiritual dimension. Those who escape from evil to good become aware of the distinction between good and evil as inspiration from Allah (JJH). The name of this stage is based on the eighth verse of Surah ash-Shams: *and inspired it (with conscience of) what is wrong for it and (what is) right for it* (91/8). *Nafs al-mulhimah* gets the power to resist the excesses of her/his desires. It moves away from anything that keeps the qalb away from Allah (JJH). Adorned with moral virtues, this nafs fulfills worship with great pleasure beyond the mere obligation of duty. The qalb becomes open to *ilham* (spiritual inspiration) since it is cleaned by the *riyazah* (abstemiousness), the *tazkiyyah* (acquitment of the heart), and the *taqwa* (piety).

Although Western psychology does not much deal with the term inspiration, receiving a message from a transcendent dimension, it put forth various explanations about the human ability of intuition, a concept close to inspiration. For example, Freud rejected intuition claiming it is unreliable and basically an illusion created to satisfy the desires (Freud 2006b: 210). On the other hand, Jung explained some of the inner abilities of the human with the term intuition by claiming that consciousness cannot produce these abilities. According to him, intuition is not what one produces, as Freud advocates. Through the collective unconscious, every person is born with an accumulation of knowledge, even if he is not aware of it. Intuition is not a situation produced by the person, but a state that occurs instinctively. If the person is fast enough, she/he catches the intuition. One knows the archetypes in the collective unconscious through intuition as well (Jung 1998: 45). Here, intuition is deeply immanent. It can be said that inspiration is the messages coming from the transcendent to the human, while intuition is the messages that the human catches from the transcendent.

The inspiration of the nafs is explained in Sufi sources as being by Allah (JJH) through angels. In this case, it can be said that conscience (wijdan) is the inner voice from the pure nature of the human (fitrah), and the inspiration is the outer voice from the angels. It is not easy to explain the fact that one is inspired by angels and Allah (JJH), namely, a transcendent dimension, with the current theories of Western psychology because many psychologists have not expressed an opinion about the ontological existence of a supreme power that transcends the human and the universe. Indeed, the possibility of such a transcendent being goes beyond the boundaries of positivistic psychology. Therefore, it is not an issue accepted by scientific psychology that the person has contact with a transcendent dimension or invisible beings such as angels or demons, which has an effect on her/his decisions. However, in Western psychology, transcendence is discussed in various ways. For instance, Maslow (1996) mentions self-transcendence while talking about self-actualization. His ideas led to transpersonal psychology, which explains different levels of consciousness using the classification of prepersonal, personal (individual), and transpersonal levels (Bidwell 1999; Wilber 1995). Moreover, the recently popular concept of spirituality in psychology literature has a similar emphasis. Generally, the definitions of spirituality refer to a belief in and a direct relationship to a higher being that goes beyond the materialistic world (see Düzgüner 2021). Also, the items such as "I believe in a Higher Power/Universal Intelligence" and "I believe there is a connection between all things that I cannot see but can sense" in spirituality scales refers to transcendence. As seen, although theories in Western psychology defend that the human can have transcendent experiences, they do not include the idea that she/he will be inspired by higher beings such as Allah (JJH)/God or angels. According to Western psychology, human development is defined as activating its own internal dynamics and achieving universal integrity. This is a kind of transcendence that the human discovers in her/his deeper psychic existence. While god, higher being,

VIEWS OF WESTERN AND ISLAMIC PSYCHOLOGY OF RELIGION 73

or ultimate truth is deeply innate in Western psychology, Allah (JJH) is both deeply innate and highly transcendent being in Islamic psychology.

4.2.4 *Nafs al-mutma'innah* (The Satisfied/Peaceful Nafs)

Nafs al-mutma'innah expresses the level of nafs dominated by a delicate balance and solemn peace, in which moral virtues are fully fulfilled. The term *mutma'innah* is used cognitively for full comprehension and complete calm. This stage has taken its name from verse twenty-seven of Surah al-Fajr: *O Nafs al-mutma'innah (satisfied nafs)! Return to your Lord well-pleased and pleasing to Him* (89/27). At the mutma'innah stage, the person resolves the conflicts of the stages of ammarah, lawwamah and mulhimah.

The person at nafs al-mutma'innah stage knows that her/his creator is Allah (JJH). They trust in Him and love Him at a high level. She/he arranges their life in the direction of Allah's (JJH) will. Religious rules and prohibitions are experienced as internalized sincere values. At this stage, the level of consciousness increases. The personal self and the spiritual self are integrated. The person is freed from the passion to have. There is no place for worldly desires but Allah (JJH) in the qalb. Divine love is increasingly experienced and negative emotions are replaced by submission to Allah (JJH). The person who came to this stage, although she/he has made some mistakes in the past, has repented them and succeeded to stand behind their repentance. She/he has shown the determination to replace the mistakes with good deeds and so their *qalb* is at peace (Ghazali 1992, v. 4: 78).

It is possible to see the investigations on a higher level of consciousness and experiences of reaching inner peace in Western psychology. With the concepts of plateau experiences, Maslow pointed to the spiritual/religious/mystical experiences that almost every person can have. Plateau experiences are more frequent and more calm experiences than the peak experiences that will be mentioned below. According to Maslow, high plateau experiences are usually emotional experiences of reaching a high mental and cognitive stage. Achieving this level of integrative consciousness is almost entirely within the will and determination of the person. Plateau experiences may become a familiar and even ordinary experience in time, still pleasing the person (Maslow 1996: 22–23). Here can be seen the shared acceptance that the human has the potential for higher levels of consciousness both in Islamic and Western psychologies. However, reaching the nafs al-mutma'innah stage does not only depend on the efforts of the person but also the blessings of Allah (JJH). Also, nafs al-mutma'innah have a deep cognitive and emotional background. According to Tasawwuf, the nafs al-mutma'innah stage is that the understanding of the Sufi sharpens and the qalb reaches peace. In the 260th verse of Surah al-Baqarah, Allah (JJH) tells the story of the Prophet Abraham (PBUH) and uses the expression of "being mutma'innah" as: *Remember, when Abraham said: "O Lord, show me how you raise the dead," He said: "Do you not believe?" "I do," answered Abraham. "I only ask for my* qalb *assurance [mutma'innah]"* (2/260). In the continuation of the verse, Allah (JJH) asks the Prophet Abraham (PBUH) to train four birds and to leave them on four separate mountains. When the Prophet Abraham (PBUH) calls them, the birds fly back to him. Allah (JJH) tells him that on the Day of Resurrection, the souls will go back to Allah (JJH) in the same way. In this request of the Prophet Abraham (PBUH), there is a desire for the qalb (heart) to be *mutma'in* (satisfied) by having a deeper understanding of something it already knows and believes in. According to the Holy Quran and Tasawwuf, the comprehension that is a result of the rise of consciousness brings inner peace. Different cognitive levels of comprehension and their relation to emotions are of an importance to be studied in psychology.

4.2.5 *Nafs ar-radhiyyah* (The Well-Pleased Nafs)

Nafs ar-radhiyyah is the stage where the person comprehends that both good and troubled events happen with the permission of Allah (JJH). So, she/he experiences complete consent via submission to Allah (JJH). *Radhiyyah* means a willingness to surrender without hesitation. This stage is named based on the twenty-seventh verse of the Surah al-Fajr: *O Nafs al-mutma'inna* [satisfied nafs]! *Return to your Lord well-pleased and well-pleasing* (89/27). In this stage, the person is grateful for the good events and is patient with the difficulties. She/he consents to Allah's (JJH) will because they know that it is Allah (JJH) who allowed them both. The person who turns to Allah (JJH) with complete surrender leaves everything except Allah (JJH), including her/his own will, and becomes union with Allah (JJH). The expression *fana fillah* is used in Tasawwuf for the experience of annihilation in the essence of Allah (JJH).

In the West, there are psychologists who discussed the experience of being one with God or the universe. For this particular experience, Maslow (1996) developed the concept of peak experiences. According to him, peak experiences are rare transcendent experiences that every person can experience. Also, they are enthusiastic and refreshing and they raise consciousness to higher levels. Peak experiences point to a state of consciousness in which the person realizes her/his full potential and perceives reality as whole. After this experience, the individual reaches their true identity and reveals her/his unique nature (Maslow 2001: 111–112). Unlike the plateau experiences, peak experiences are in the form of a sudden leap in awareness, and rarely occur.

However, the effects of it can be permanent. Such experiences are often described as a kind of rebirth. These can be experienced by everyone at any unexpected place and time. Peak experiences include intense emotional experiences, awe, integration, and values that are now experienced beyond being aware of them (Maslow 1996: 22–23).

Maslow considers all of them as peak experiences without any distinction between experiences such as revelation experience, enlightenment, access to Nirvana, or feeling of being one with the transcendent. Transpersonal psychology, which is based on the principle of individual transformation by reaching the upper levels of consciousness, frequently focuses on the stage where complete peace of mind is achieved as well. According to this school, when one stands out from all the limiting identifications at the deepest level of the soul, consciousness feels beyond the boundaries of space and time. This experience is labeled as "pure awareness," "everything," and "nothing," "all universe," "independent from conditions," "constant," "infinite" and "unity with others" or "unity with God" (Walsh and Vaughan 2001: 76). This point is where the human reaches their true self. God represents the direct experience of all beings (Bidwell 1999: 87).

As can be seen, psychologists also talked about the balance and inner harmony, one has reached in the inner world, the experience of being one with God, or the stage of enlightenment. They dealt with this issue as a natural experience, pointed out by all mystical traditions. The nafs al-mutma'innah stage in Tasawwuf is similar to the psychological approaches to the mystical experience in terms of pointing to a higher level of consciousness and intense inner peace. However, while talking about this personal experience, psychologists have clearly criticized the institutional and dogmatic structure of religion. Moreover, they have claimed that religious structure is an obstacle to the mystical/spiritual awakening of individuals. According to them, reaching peak experiences is a conscious initiative that is not based on dogmas and is based on personal experience, not the authority of religious tradition or divine inspiration. Every person has this ability. Peak experiences of the prophets, saints, or ordinary people are the result of this natural development (Barnard 2000: 309).

Tasawwuf also accepts that such transcendental experiences are a natural feature of human beings, but there is the nuance that separates the prophetic experience in Islam from the peak experiences of other people. By purifying her/his nafs, a person can rise spiritually and gain higher consciousness. However, prophecy is not just a stage to be reached by one's own spiritual development. Prophets are people chosen by Allah (JJH). In other words, in prophecy, there is both an internal orientation toward Allah (JJH) and being chosen by Him. For this reason, prophets are not only people who tell others the knowledge they have gained in the light of their own experiences. Indeed, they are those who convey Allah's (JJH) messages to the people.

Additionally, the relationship between the human and Allah (JJH) in Tasawwuf does not resemble the Western humanistic psychological view of God. The above-mentioned psychological approaches regard God only as an essence in the human and explain the experience of reaching God with meeting one's own real identity. This approach sounds similar to the principle of Tasawwuf: "who knows her/himself knows her/his Lord." However, in Islam, Allah (JJH) is the creator of the universes and is also very close to the human: *He created man and surely know what misdoubts arise in their qalbs; We are closer to him than his jugular vein* (50/16). In Western psychology, God is only an immanent being, while in Tasawwuf, Allah (JJH) is both immanent and transcendent being.

Here we would like to note the different approaches to transcendence. A glance at the psychological literature on spirituality, self-actualization, higher level of consciousness, and peak experiences will see the term 'transcendence' that refers to going beyond the daily consciousness. Transcendence is related to inner awaking and the experience of rebirth. This type of transcendence is still immanent to the human, namely two-dimensional. The acceptance of this type of transcendence in psychology literature shows that an absolute materialistic and positivistic approach to the human has been criticized and that alternative explanations that go beyond them have been presented. However, the transcendence in Islam includes this two-dimensional immanent transcendence and gets to the third dimension since it depends on the truth of the active influence of Allah (JJH) (Iqbal and Skinner 2021; Utz 2011). According to Western psychology, the human disposes of her/his own masks and reaches their own self, and according to Tasawwuf, the human disposes of their own self and reaches Allah (JJH). So, Islamic psychology investigates both immanent two-dimensional transcendent and divine three-dimensional transcendent experiences.

4.2.6   *Nafs al-mardhiyyah* (The Well-Pleasing Nafs)

Nafs al-mardhiyyah is the stage in which mutual consent is experienced between Allah (JJH) and the servant. *Mardhiyyah* means "being pleased" and indicates that Allah (JJH) is pleased with the person at this stage. Like the previous stage, nafs al-mardhiyyah is named based on the twenty-seventh verse of the Surah al-Fajr: *O Nafs al-mutma'inna* [satisfied nafs]! *Return to your Lord*

VIEWS OF WESTERN AND ISLAMIC PSYCHOLOGY OF RELIGION 77

well-pleased and well-pleasing (89/27). At this level, the person has no desire other than remembrance of Allah (JJH). This spiritually developed and morally transformed nafs loves all creatures and shows tenderness to them, seeing a manifestation of Him. Universal thought has developed, and consciousness has extended beyond this world.

Western psychological theories make explanations of the human experience of being one with God, transcendent being, the universe, or true essence within her/himself. These explanations mostly assert this experience as a top stage of personal enlightenment/awakening/nirvana or whatever they term it. The experience of becoming union with Allah (JJH) is called fana fillah in Tasawwuf, as stated above. Hence, this is not the last stage in spiritual development. The spiritual transformation goes further, as seen in the stage of nafs al-mardhiyyah and the following *kamilah*. So, Western psychology theories have not discussed an experience similar to nafs al-mardhiyyah and kamilah yet.

4.2.7   *Nafs al-kamilah* (The Mature/Perfect Nafs)

Nafs al-kamilah is the stage to reach full maturity in a spiritual sense. The Sufis have classified six stages based on the Holy Quran and add the last stage to point to the full spiritual maturity. At this level, the nafs becomes totally pure. The person is filled with divine love and all the "I/He" distinctions have disappeared; they become one with Allah (JJH) and can preserve this experience. The person at this level gained all the ingenuity features and rose to the position of spiritual guidance to those who are at the beginning of the path of spiritual purification.

According to Tasawwuf, there is a natural tendency within every human being toward psychospiritual transformation by shining the mirror of the qalb. However, Sufis (mureed) who are on the path of self-purification go through these stages in the company of a guide (*sheikh*). A sheikh is a person who has reached the stage of nafs al-kamilah. The sheikh guides the dervish in various ways, taking into account their abilities, personality traits, mood, and temperament, and observes their experiences. These experiences are basically divided into two as *hal* (state) and *maqam* (station). Hal refers to the temporary mood swings that most Sufis experience. It can be said that it is the form of daily mood changes in the Sufi way, which is also used as a state of mind. There are various emotional states, such as *khauf* and *raja'* (fear and hope), and *qabz* and *bast* (boredom and relief). Maqam, on the other hand, indicates a permanent level of transformation rather than a variable psychological state. The fact that the Sufi reaches a certain rank means that there has been a structural change in their ruh, and the person has reached a different level of consciousness. The basic maqams are tawbah (repentance), *zuhd* (asceticism), and *reza* (consent) (Küçük 2011). The sheikh uses different methods in certain proportions while guiding the mureed, such as: *halwah* (stand alone with Allah [JJH]), *tafakkur* (thinking about Allah [JJH]), *sawm* (fasting), *riyazah* (limiting worldly needs), *dhikr* (repeating the name of Allah [JJH] by heart), and salah (prayer). Studies and research on the psychological effects of these experiences and methods are still ongoing.

∙∙∙

In conclusion, it can be said that both Tasawwuf and psychology recognize that the human has the potential and abilities to develop her/himself. Both speak of the existence of the lower and upper layers of human consciousness. Both acknowledge that it is important for human self-improvement to be able to establish healthy communication in their relations with others as well as personal awareness. Both of them deal with the thoughts, emotions, and behaviors of people and explain the causes and consequences that push the person to this behavior in their own system. While psychology aims to analyze the human as it is, Islam and Tasawwuf offers a roadmap to what kind of person it ought to be, as well as telling the person that it is important to know her/himself.

The spiritual development in Tasawwuf encompasses this world and beyond. The mission of the person is to control her/his nafs, to polish the mirror of the qalb, and to taste the joy of reaching Allah (JJH). These experiences are among the subjects of Islamic and Sufi psychology. Hence, here is the point where psychology and theology are separated from each other. Here we would like to note the borders of the fields of Tasawwuf and Islamic/Sufi psychology. The personal transformation side of this model forms the basis of Islamic and Sufi psychology. Studying these experiences from an Islamic perspective draws the borders of Islamic psychology. Investigating these experiences depending on Sufi teachings draws the borders of Sufi psychology. The higher-level spiritual knowledge side of this model belongs to Islamic theology and Tasawwuf. It seems that as a rapidly growing area, Islamic psychology will enwiden its study area and will reveal its own subbranches, such as depending on specific culture or madhab. In this process, Islamic psychology needs to make clearer its borders with theology and Tasawwuf as well as other psychologies. What follows is an example that points at the basic boundaries of the Islamic view of the human, based on Rumi's explanations.

VIEWS OF WESTERN AND ISLAMIC PSYCHOLOGY OF RELIGION 79

4.3 *Complementary Views on Selected Stories from Rumi's* **Mathnawi**

Mawlana Jalaladdin Rumi (d. 1273) was a Muslim scholar, Sufi, poet, and interpreter of the Holy Quran. He has been one of the most well-known Sufis all over the world for centuries. His masterpieces underline tolerance, reasoning, compassion, goodness, love, and the like. Containing many correct determinations on the human being, his thoughts have great potential to contribute to psychology today.

Rumi's masterpiece *Mathnawi-i Ma'nawi* is written as a poem that tells some stories. Each character in these stories has a symbolic meaning. He also explains the analogy and the lessons to be learned at the ends of the stories. *Mathnawi* starts with the story of *nay* (reed) which symbolizes human beings. The second story, of the sultan and the handmaid, explains the meaning of life and presents a way of life. He tells stories about human nature as well. For instance, Mawlana very well expressed the harmful potential of the nafs, which cannot be completely eradicated, with the story of a dragon hunter. He answers the question of why evil exists via the story of a conversation between the Prophet Moses (PBUH) and Allah (JJH). On the other hand, he underlines the importance and necessity of prosocial behaviors in the story about the young man and thorns. In sum, he presents a complementary perspective to psychology about human nature and relationships with others and Allah (JJH)/God/Higher Being.

4.3.1 The Story of Nay

> Listen to the reed how it tells a tale, complaining of separations
> Saying, "Ever since I was parted from the reed-bed,
> my lament hath caused man and woman to moan.
> I want a bosom torn by severance, that I may unfold (to such
> a one) the pain of love-desire.
> Everyone who is left far from his source wishes back the
> time when he was united with it.
> In every company I uttered my wailful notes, I consorted
> with the unhappy and with them that rejoice.
> Everyone became my friend from his own opinion; none
> sought out my secrets from within me.
> My secret is not far from my plaint, but ear and eye lack the
> light (whereby it should be apprehended).
> Body is not veiled from soul, nor soul from body, yet none is
> permitted to see the soul.

This noise of the reed is fire, it is not wind: whoso hath not
this fire, may he be naught!
'Tis the fire of Love that is in the reed, 'tis the fervour of
Love that is in the wine.
The reed is the comrade of everyone who has been parted
from a friend: its strains pierced our hearts.
Who ever saw a poison and antidote like the reed? Whoever
saw a sympathiser and a longing lover like the reed?
The reed tells of the Way full of blood and recounts stories of
the passion of Majnún.
Only to the senseless is this sense confided: the tongue hath
no customer save the ear.
In our woe the days (of life) have become untimely: our
days travel hand in hand with burning griefs.
If our days are gone, let them go! – 'tis no matter. Do Thou
remain, for none is holy as Thou art!
Whoever is not a fish becomes sated with His water; whoever
is without daily bread finds the day long.
None that is raw understands the state of the ripe:
Therefore my words must be brief. Farewell!

Mathnawi, v. 1, c.1–18[5]

Rumi describes life as a spiritual journey with the metaphor of nay (reed). Nay
has been detached from its motherland and become an instrument. It is wistful because of this separation. Like nay, people are far from their homeland
(the eternal world) here on this earth. With the spiritual practices of Tasawwuf,
she/he can experience reunification. So, Tasawwuf does not contain only a theory but also experiences and practices.

This story succinctly describes the Islamic model of the human. This world
is not the homeland of the human, she/he is in exile in this world. Therefore,
all the happiness and sorrow experienced here is temporary. Life is a road that
stretches to infinity and the world is like a station where some time is spent.
The human intuitively realizes that she/he came from another world and seeks
that ultimate truth. This quest is basically divine love. However, only those
who have reached a higher level of consciousness will understand this, not
those who have remained in the raw nature. The more a person purifies her/his
nafs, the more deeply is divine love felt.

---

5 These eighteen couplets were translated by R.A. Nicholson.

VIEWS OF WESTERN AND ISLAMIC PSYCHOLOGY OF RELIGION   81

Rumi also explained the departure of the human from this world by likening death to the wedding night. The definition of death as a night of happiness is because it symbolizes the transience of worldly life and the moment of meeting Allah (JJH), the beloved one. Rumi stated that death is not a reason for fear, but a moment of confrontation for those who have completed their maturation in this world, saying, "Are the mature walnuts afraid of being broken?" Thus, he explained that people come to this world from an eternal one with the metaphor of nay, and that they should spend their worldly life by maturing themselves with the metaphor of walnuts, and that people leave this world to meet their lover with the metaphor of the wedding night. This is the basis of the human model of Islam. Thus, Islamic psychology provides a unique explanation to the existence of the human, suggests a lifelong transformation process that gives meaning and purpose to life, and presents a coping strategy with the troubles in life including fear of death.

4.3.2   The Sultan and the Handmaid

A sultan (king) went hunting and saw a handmaid in a village. He fell in love with her. He took the girl to his palace and they got married. But after marriage, something went bad. The sultan was happy, but the young lady got sick. The sultan called all the doctors in his country to treat his beloved wife, they tried many different methods but all failed. The sultan begged Allah (JJH) a lot. As he was tired and fell asleep, he dreamed of an old man who heralded that a stranger would come the next day and heal his wife. When the sultan awoke, he began to wait for the stranger. Once the sultan saw him from a distance, he understood he is the healer. They felt as if they knew each other. The healer started to take the pulse of the lady. At the same time, he asked her to tell her life in the village. She started to talk about her family and other people in her hometown. While she was talking about a jeweler the doctor realized that her pulse increased. At the end of the session he found out that the lady had fallen in love with the jeweler, but the sultan took her to his palace. Since she missed her beloved jeweler a lot, she got sick. The doctor told the sultan to bring the jeweler and let the lady marry him. Six months later the healer secretly gave a syrup to the jeweler, which made him weak and ugly. Then the lady fell out of love. Thus, she got well. Meanwhile, the sultan realized that what he really needs is a perfect guide who shows the right path to him.

Mathnawi, v. 1, *c.*35–79

Rumi called this story "our story" because it symbolizes the journey of human in this world. The sultan is the ruh. The handmaid symbolizes the nafs al-ammarah. The jewelry is the worldly desires such as making much money, having houses, cars, high positions, etc. Mawlana Rumi says that as human beings we fell in love with this world but this world loves gold, jewel, money, and so on. The healer symbolizes the *insan-i kameel* (the mature human), the guide who shows the human being what real love is, what is the main mission of human being in this world.

This story explains the Islamic understanding of life in general. The human should focus on spiritual peace, not earthly desires. Real love, real success, and the real world are not those in this world but the eternal. This does not mean not to take this world into consideration. Here is a significant difference. Trying to make money and the desire to make money are different from each other. Neither Muslims nor Sufis isolate themselves from social life entirely, as seen in other mystical traditions. The Islamic model of the human covers all people. That is why it penetrates every moment of life, namely an ordinary life. What Rumi warns against is being addicted to the world and the love of worldly things in the heart. Having money or a high position is good to make charity as well. All is about the heart, not physical wealth. The desires are harmful to the person since it strengthens the selfish ego. The human has a natural tendency to higher purposes, as seen when the sultan feels close to the healer who calls for divine love. Islamic psychology underlines tending to the transcendent by leaving egoistic and narcissistic addictions.

4.3.3 Allah (JJH) and the Prophet Moses (PBUH)

One day, the Prophet Moses (PBUH) asked Allah (JJH): "why do you create such beauties and then destroy them?" Allah (JJH)answered: "I know you did not ask this because of your denial or negligence, you are asking to learn the wisdom and to let people know. The question arises from knowledge, and so does the answer. Just as the rose and the thorn come out of the mud. Going astray and entering the right path both come from knowledge. So, plant a crop on the earth and find out the answer." The prophet Moses (PBUH) planted the crop. The crops grew. After they had matured well, he took the sickle and mowed them. At this moment, Allah (JJH) asked him: "You planted it well, you brought it up, but when it matured, why did you reap it?" "O Lord, there is both wheat and straw here. I do it so as not to mix the two." Then Allah (JJH) said: "Among the creatures are both pure spirits and those covered with mud. Just as it is

VIEWS OF WESTERN AND ISLAMIC PSYCHOLOGY OF RELIGION

necessary to separate the wheat from the chaff, it is necessary to separate the good from the bad." This universe was created in order to uncover the treasure of wisdom. Allah (JJH) said: "I was a hidden treasure." Listen to this and do not lose your ore but uncover it.

Mathnawi, v. 4, c.3004–3030

In this story, Rumi explains the evils and difficulties faced by the human. This story recalls a hadith of the Prophet Muhammad (PBUH):

The example of a believer is that of a fresh green plant the leaves of which move in whatever direction the wind forces them to move and when the wind becomes still, it stands straight. Such is the similitude of the believer: He is disturbed by calamities (but is like the fresh plant he regains his normal state soon). And the example of a disbeliever is that of a pine tree (which remains) hard and straight till Allah (JJH) cuts it down when He will.

BUKHARI, Tawheed, 31

This story and hadith also describe the attitude of the human toward the difficulties encountered in the journey of life. Rumi's story and the hadith of the prophet explain coping processes from an Islamic perspective. Belief provides people with psychological and spiritual resilience. The idea that the difficulties of this world are temporary gives endurance to the human. The idea that difficulties are the time to separate the good from the bad allows one to turn difficulties into a success of purification and gaining strength. No matter how great the difficulties, the belief that a person who believes in Allah (JJH) will eventually overcome them also gives endurance. Thus, the difficulties take on a new meaning, the third dimension. Because overcoming this difficulty means getting one step closer to Allah (JJH) the difficulty can turn into a spiritual gain.

Even if a person has psychological stress when she/he experiences difficulties such as illness, failure, low income, then they can maintain spiritual well-being with the thought that Allah (JJH) is with them and that they will receive blessings at the end of this process. Because each difficulty can turn into a blessing depending on the individual's attitude toward it. Similarly, blessings such as money, possessions, and high position can also turn into tests. So, if a person stops remembering Allah (JJH) when they are successful, healthy, or rich and does not help others, these seemingly good conditions are a test. If these tests push a person to act selfishly, arrogantly, and ambitiously, these blessings become a challenge for that person. In other words, the events that happen to a person become a challenge or a blessing depending on the person's reaction to it. A person who believes in Allah (JJH) and who is always connected to Him is grateful when she/he is well, and she/he is resistant in the face of difficulties.

4.3.4 The Dragon Hunter

A snake-hunter was looking for a huge snake, a dragon, in the snowy mountains. He found a huge dead snake that even the shape of it was terrifying. He decided to make money by showing it to people and dragged it to Baghdad. He told the people, "I brought a dead dragon, how hard I hunted it," but he was wrong because the dragon was not dead, just frozen from the cold. Hearing the man's words, the people gathered around in curiosity. The man waited for more people to gather. At last, the snake-hunter pretended to open the rug on the tethered and frozen dragon. The snake-hunter had carefully tied the dragon with ropes but did not open the rugs for more people to come. When the sun's rays hit, the warming snake began to move, and the people began to flee in fear. Hearing the voices of the people, the dragon stood up and broke off its ropes. While fleeing, the people crushed each other, and many died. The snake-hunter stood aghast saying "I had brought a lot of trouble." If Pharaoh gets this power, he will hinder hundreds of Moses and Harun. But that dragon will be a tiny worm in the hands of poverty. You are safe when your dragon is frozen, but if it is free you will be bait for it. Defeat it before it defeats you. Do not pity it, it is not the person to be favored. Keep your dragon in the snow of separation, do not let it touch the sun of desires. Do you hope to keep it well-behaved, relaxed, and loyal without any torment? You need a Moses to kill the dragon. Thousands of people were defeated by their dragon and died away!

Mathnawi, v. 3, c.975–1065

As narrated in the story, the nafs can drag people to disaster as long as it is not taken under control. The nafs is the aspect that enables the existence and survival of people in this world, but it also includes the part that directs people to extremism. Therefore, it is not possible to completely dismantle and dispose of this side of the human, but it is possible to train it to reach higher levels of consciousness Interestingly, some famous books and movies use almost the same metaphor as Rumi. The book and movie *Life of Pi* revolves around learning

VIEWS OF WESTERN AND ISLAMIC PSYCHOLOGY OF RELIGION 85

to control a tiger. In the movie *Avatar*, the character learns how to control a dragon. Also, there is a computer-animated film *How to Train Your Dragon*. In all of these, the animals are a part of humans. It seems like many people realized that there is a wild side of the human that needs to be controlled and trained. However, in Islamic psychology nafs is not just a wild selfish nature that needs to be controlled but a significant vehicle to reach Allah (JJH) via purification.

4.3.5 The Young Man and Thorns

There was a sweet-talking but bad-tempered man. He had planted a bush on the road. The passers-by began to get harmed and told him to uproot these thorny bushes, but he just ignored them. The bushes were growing more and more, people's feet and hands were bleeding because of the thorns, and people's clothes were caught in the bushes and torn. They reported this to the governor, and he ordered the man repeatedly: "Remove these bushes." He was saying "Okay, I'll take it out one day" but he was delaying the work by saying "Tomorrow tomorrow." Over time, the bushes grew and took root. One day the governor said, "Do not delay the work I have ordered." The man answered, "Sir, there is a lot of time, if not today, I will do it tomorrow." The governor replied, "No, hurry up. The thorn is growing and getting stronger, but you are getting older and weaker." Be aware that every bad habit of yours as a thorn. Not only others but also you will be destroyed by your wrong actions.

Mathnawi, v. 2, c.1227–1247

This story explains that a human's bad habits harm not only her/himself but also those around her/him. In other words, according to Islam, a person's life is not just about her/himself. Purification of the nafs cannot be achieved by staying alone and focusing on deep inner experiences. The human model of Islam is holistic and encompasses the individual, social, and spiritual dimensions of human. Therefore, in order to be purified, one must also behave well toward other people and living things. These issues are currently being studied in the field of social psychology. The human is an entity that affects and is affected by her/his environment. Therefore, it is important to establish healthy social relationships. In addition, the approach of positive psychology today is also included in this story. Virtues such as altruism, helping, and forgiveness have positive effects on a person's psychological well-being. Getting rid of the thorns in the story means quitting bad habits. These are described as diseases of the heart in Islamic psychology. One should get rid of these diseases as soon as possible, because disorders such as narcissism and addiction become difficult to overcome over time. This is important both for one's own happiness and for healthy communication with those around them. Thus, she/he will feel spiritual peace as well.

•••

In sum, it can be said that just these five stories selected from Rumi's *Mathnawi* are sufficient to understand the human model of Islam. According to this, the human – like a nay – came to this world from the eternal realm and will return there again. As seen in the sultan's story, even though the raw nature of man has worldly ambitions, she/he intuitively feels that she/he has higher goals and goes in search of them. In order to achieve these goals, she/he needs to purify her/himself and reach the upper levels of consciousness. As seen in the snake-hunter story, the nafs can be controlled but not destroyed, because it is the essence of life. In order to control and purify the nafs, the person must overcome various difficulties. As in the story of the Prophet Moses (PBUH), all kinds of difficulties and blessings can turn into a gain or a problem according to one's choices. A person's nafs is not only purified by her/his personal experiences but they also need to develop themselves socially. As in the story of the young man and the thorns, healthy communication with other living things is a part of the personal purification process. In Islamic psychology, it is essential to maintain a balance in the communication that a person establishes with her/himself, their environment, and Allah (JJH), since mental, social, and spiritual dimensions affect each other. According to Islamic psychology, well-being and happiness mean having a balanced personality in these three dimensions, which means holistic health.

4.4 Complementary Views on Physical, Psychosocial, and Spiritual Health

Medical science that aims to offer health services includes different techniques and applications depending on the civilization in which it operates. The definitions of the concepts of health and disease/disorder also differ according to these civilizations. Therefore, there are similarities and divergences between the modern health understanding of Western civilization and the health understanding of all non-Western civilizations in general and Islamic civilization in particular. Today, there is also an interest in the medical practices of different civilizations.

The modern science of the Western civilization that emerged as a result of the Enlightenment put forth a new approach to this world. This approach, the mechanical view of the universe, gave rise to the mechanical view of the human. The idea that the human is not acted upon by an invisible being such as the soul, but that the human is a being under the influence of biochemical processes, formed the basis of modern medicine. Thus, modern medical applications were developed, such as medication, surgery, and organ transplantation, which are practiced all over the world today.

Medical practices in non-Western countries, on the other hand, have a background just as the emergence of psychology. These countries had an understanding and practice of medicine based on their own culture and history; afterward, Western-based modern medicine came to these countries. Thus, while the new medicine was defined as "modern medicine," the existing medical practices in these countries and based on their own civilizations were defined as "traditional medicine." Although many hospitals based on modern medicine were established, previous medical practices continued to exist in these countries. An example of this is moxibustion, "ancient Chinese medicine using bian stone (needle stone) as an instrument for the treatment of diseases" (Liangyue 2001), which is still practiced in the Far East countries.

Moreover, modern medicine spreading from the West to the rest of the world has begun to take an interest in and even apply these traditional practices. The incorporation of acupuncture therapy from Chinese medicine as a unit in modern hospitals today is an example of the interaction of Western and non-Western medicine in physical health practices. A similar situation is also valid for Islamic civilization. Since Islamic countries are spread over a wide area, there are a wide variety of health applications. The Prophet Muhammad's (PBUH) medical practices, *tibb ul-nabawi*, is a common point of all. Although its history dates back to earlier times than the period of the prophet, *hajamat* (cupping) (Şeker 2013) is still a common practice in Muslim countries, since he practiced it. Just like acupuncture, hajamat has recently started to be applied in hospitals that provide health services based on modern medicine.

The body-oriented practices of Chinese medicine are based on the understanding of the body and health in that civilization. According to Chinese medicine, the human body has an energy area surrounding the body. The energies called Yin and Yang extend to the meridians stretching between earth and sky, and these meridians are associated with the human veins. The dimension beyond the human body is also included in medicine. Just as every vein in the human body is related to the celestial bodies, the nerves passing through the ear of the human are also related to the organs in the body. Organs can be treated by stimulating these nerves in the ear. There is such an understanding of the body behind the technique of acupuncture (Kavaklı 2010). Medical practices in Islamic civilization are also based on the body understanding prevailing in these areas. The generally accepted approach is the theory of four humors (*akhlat-i arba'a*). The health of the body depends on the balance of the four humors in the body in the form of blood, phlegm, yellow bile, and black bile. If there is an increase or decrease in one of these fluids, health will deteriorate. Hajamat (Benli 2017) is the practice of pulling out the harmful redundant fluids from the body with medical intervention.

Civilizations have different understandings, even for the structures that can be seen and examined like the body. Similarly, Western and non-Western cultures have different approaches and practices in psychological health practices. In order to understand how Western and Islamic psychologies explain the concept of psychological health, it is necessary to know the explanations of these two approaches on the functioning of the invisible dimension of human beings, namely the psyche.

In the nineteenth century, while research on the human body was continuing in Western modern science, the concept of the soul left its place in the concept of mind as stated in the first chapter. Until the 1990s, health was defined as a person's physical, mental, and social well-being. Based on this, it can be said that the human being was handled in two dimensions: the physical dimension of the human body, and the psychological dimension consisting of mental and social activities. Therefore, in general, health was defined as a person's physiological and psychological well-being, and health services regarding these two dimensions were provided. In modern medicine, the human body was explained by systems such as muscles, bones, and nerves, and if these systems did not work harmoniously, medical diagnosis and treatment processes were put into action. On the other hand, psychology emerged to examine the invisible activities of human beings such as emotions, thoughts, and attitudes, while psychological counseling and psychotherapy aim to treat mental disorders, and psychiatry aims to solve advanced mental disorders with drug treatment.

After the 1990s, research on religion and spirituality clearly showed that human beings also have a spiritual dimension. Thereupon, the World Health Organization (1998) changed the definition of health to "physical, mental, social, and spiritual well-being." The same institution included the spiritual dimension in the Quality of Life Scale and addressed spirituality as a requirement of quality of life. This new definition and scale gave a serious impetus to studies on the spiritual dimension. Today, many countries, especially Western

VIEWS OF WESTERN AND ISLAMIC PSYCHOLOGY OF RELIGION   89

countries, provide spiritual care and counseling services in institutions such as hospitals, schools, the army, nursing homes, and prisons. In other words, spiritual care practices are included in health care services.

On the other hand, the understanding of health in Islam is in the form of physical and spiritual health. Islamic literature is full of the practices of many physicians on physical health, especially the great physicians Ibn Sina and Razi. In the human model of Islam, the qalb may be healthy or ill just like the body. A healthy qalb means that a person is generally happy and peaceful. Since Islam is defined as a religion that provides happiness in this world and the hereafter, the subject of happiness has been frequently discussed in the literature.

Muslim scholars and thinkers published many studies on happiness, the ultimate goal of psychology and psychotherapy today. In fact, books with names such as *Ways to Get Rid of Sadness*, *Guide to Happiness*, or *Success* are usually in the personal development section of big bookstores today. However, *Ways to Get Rid of Sadness (al-Hila li-dafʿ il-ahzan)* is a book by Kindi, *Guide to Happiness (Kimya as-saʿadah)* was written by Ghazali, and *Success (an-Najat)* is a book by Ibn Sina, all of whom lived between the ninth and twelfth centuries. In the Islamic tradition, health and happiness are generally defined as "avoiding all kinds of extremes and being virtuous."

Disruptions in the functioning of the body cause bodily diseases, while the qalb's malfunctioning causes qalb diseases. The general definition of health in Islam is based on avoiding extremes and maintaining balance. In other words, it is accepted that just as overeating will cause bodily problems, excessive anger will also cause qalb disease. Diseases of the qalb are not limited to mental illnesses of Western psychology. Throughout the Islamic tradition, psychological disorders such as stress, anxiety, uncontrolled anger, and narcissistic personality, which are in the field of psychology today, have been evaluated together with morally wrong attitudes such as self-indulgence, jealousy, and lying. For example, Kindi thought that demands arising from the pressures of basic emotions and passions, such as uncontrolled anger and lust, as well as pathological manifestations, such as sadness, anxiety, and fear of death, which are expressions of unhappiness, will also prevent human moral competence. Similarly, Razi dealt with various bad habits and tendencies of the nafs, such as pleasure-sorrow relationship, lustful love, self-love, envy, lies, stinginess, extreme anger, drink addiction, greed, sadness, and fear of death.

In general, Islamic sources deal with the human in two ways: the material side and the psychospiritual side. The material aspect of the human is the body. Health services in this direction are also described as material medicine (*tibb ul-jismani*). The psychospiritual side of the human, on the other hand, covers the mental and spiritual aspects of modern psychology. Health services related to this aspect of the human are also described as spiritual medicine (*tibb ur-ruhani*). For this reason, spiritual references and practices are frequently included in the study of the psychological aspect of human beings. Indeed, physiological health, psychological well-being, and moral virtues are intertwined. Therefore, it is almost synonymous to be physically healthy, psychologically happy, and spiritually peaceful in Islamic psychology.

The fact that Islamic psychology considers moral virtues such as forgiveness, helping, and gratitude to be necessary for the health of the qalb is in line with today's positive psychology research. It has been revealed that attitudes such as arrogance and jealousy lead to personality disorders such as narcissism. Recently, Western psychology has tended to investigate spirituality and values. Therefore, Western and Islamic psychologies are getting closer to each other.

Today, Western psychology offers many theories, research, and psychotherapy applications to improve the quality of life. Like other non-Western countries, Islamic countries also benefit from this accumulation. At the same time, the Islamic psychology approach gains interest. Western and Islamic approaches have a relationship based on mutual contribution in the field of psychology as well as in the field of medicine. For example, a Muslim who is sick in her/his body not only applies medicine and surgery but also recites healing verses from the Holy Quran by placing her/his hand on the aching place, as the Prophet Muhammad (PBUH) did. Today, in the field of psychology, besides other therapy techniques, applications in Islamic literature are also used. While people are coping with psychological stress, they also get support from Islamic sources.

Traditional medicine practices did not disappear when modern medicine emerged. On the contrary, these practices are now integrated into modern medicine. The theory, research, and practice of Western and Islamic psychologies have a similar interaction. An explanation can be made to make the picture clearer. What is done in the West today is the integration of spiritual elements into the field of psychology. In Islamic literature, what is done is to determine the psychological elements in the field of spirituality.

Although their theoretical backgrounds are different, the common point in Western and Islamic psychologies is that human beings have a spiritual dimension as well as their physical, mental, and social dimensions. The physical, psychosocial, and spiritual dimensions of the human are in interaction with each other. For example, if the individual experiences a state of sadness for a long time, this situation may reflect on his body, such as with headaches and stomachaches. In other words, a psychological problem may be felt physiologically. Similarly, a positive state experienced by a person in the spiritual dimension, such as praying, will also reflect positively on her/his psychology, because if praying means turning to Allah (JJH) and communicating with Him, feeling the presence and support of a supreme power will help the person to calm down. Therefore, it can be said that the human is a whole consisting of different dimensions and these dimensions are in interaction with each other. The individual needs expert support in solving the problems that arise in these dimensions.

It should be underlined here that the main problem in Islamic psychology publications is the confusion between psychological health and spiritual health. Since spiritual stress leads to psychological problems such as depression, some scholars regard spiritual problems as psychological problems. Likewise, spiritual treatment is being mixed with psychological treatment. It is true that reading the Holy Quran makes people calm and peaceful, but solely reading it does not solve psychological problems. Here is one of our witnessed cases. A young lady was diagnosed with a personality and eating disorder as a result of family problems. She turned into a skinny girl in several months. Since she was a religious person, she believed in reading the Holy Quran as a remedy for her. Then she started to read it, perform salah, and repeat the name of Allah (*dhikr*) more and more. But nothing changed. After a while, she started to feel disappointed and to say "I have been worshipping Allah (JJH) as much as I can, but He never helps me." Then she started to feel more anxious and to be afraid of losing her faith. She already had psychological stress and then she developed spiritual stress as well.

As can be seen in the above example, psychology-based problems cannot be solved by spirituality-based practices. What is worse is that some clients may tend to religious practices to escape from the source of their psychological problems. In psychotherapy, the first step is to admit the problem, that is, to be brave enough to face the problem. There are many cognitive strategies to ignore the problem. The therapist should be aware of these cognitive traps in the mind of the client and should encourage her/him not to ignore the problem. Religious practices should not be a way to escape from the problem. So Islamic psychology studies and applications should be very sensitive.

We suggest a classification to allow sensitive studies (Figure 11). The human being has three dimensions: (1) the physical dimension points to the body; (2) the psychosocial dimension points to thoughts, emotions, and behaviors; and (3) the spiritual dimension points to purpose/meaning in life, values, and belief in a higher being.

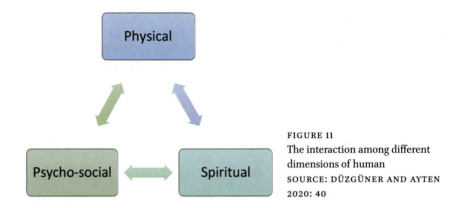

FIGURE 11　The interaction among different dimensions of human
SOURCE: DÜZGÜNER AND AYTEN 2020: 40

Physical problems can be solved by physicians, psychosocial problems can be solved by psychologists and psychiatrists, and spiritual problems can be solved by spiritual counselors. All these dimensions interact with each other, but they cannot take the place of the other. A problem that arises in the psychological dimension cannot be solved by strengthening the spiritual dimension, and vice versa. For this reason, understanding that psychological counseling and spiritual counseling complement each other is important in terms of a holistic approach to human beings. Islamic psychology, which combines spirituality and psychology, is a good example of this holistic approach. The Islamic understanding of the human includes all these three dimensions as a whole, so it is not easy to draw clear boundaries between/among those. It is possible to contribute to the literature if we undertake sensitive and detailed studies though, as we tried to point out in the complementary method.

5　Conclusion

Western and Islamic psychologies' views of the human are the result of the historical flow of each. While the psychological issues were part of religion and philosophy initially, psychology became an independent discipline as a result of the paradigm shift in Europe in the seventeenth century. The Western paradigm has been an effort to establish a science independent of religion and philosophy, which disables or even ignores the spiritual and metaphysical. Although some schools of thought adopted this approach, the psychology of religion and religious psychology have always existed in the literature of Western psychology. Even more, recently there has been a shift in interest from material to non-material. For instance, invisible art attracts more attention today. Artworks that do not exist in the physical realm but are thought to exist as an experience find buyers at very high prices. Also, the virtual world is now a part of the physical realm. People exist in the digital world and metaverse with various accounts and avatars. Moreover, they can shop in the physical world with the money belonging to the virtual world. These virtual activities lead to the acceptance of the existence of phenomena that do not exist in the physical world. When we consider developments such as quantum physics and black holes, metaphysics actually knocks on the door of positivistic science. Hence, Western psychology is undergoing a transition toward the existence of the invisible, with the acceptance of the spiritual dimension as well as the physical, mental, and social dimensions of the human being.

On the other hand, Islamic psychology offers a model of the human based on the Holy Quran and hadiths and enriched by Muslim scholars. This model has both ideological and practical roots in history. It is a fact that there were deteriorations in institutions in Islamic countries due to historical, social, and political developments. However, the holistic approach to the human has continued to exist as wisdom independent of institutions in all Islamic countries. Islam covers all periods from the first man and the first prophet Adam (PBUH) to the last prophet Muhammad (PBUH). Muslim scholars, leaders, artists, architects produced a deep-rooted accumulation of thought, science, art, literature, and architecture from the time of the Prophet Muhammad (PBUH) to the present. The Islamic perspective is basically an inclusive understanding that is enriched with different times and cultures by having common points. The watercolor brush pen is a good metaphor to explain this. Water makes each pen a different color. Islam is the water and colors are the cultures. Islam makes each culture a different feature, but the same background. Islam draws a general frame about the human being. Cultures and individuals fill this frame on their own. Moreover, this frame is not limited to Muslims. Islamic understanding, in which physics and metaphysics, the material and the spiritual are considered as a whole, has a model that deals with the human, the universe, and Allah (JJH) together. Islamic psychology is also based on this model and continues to enrich by incorporating the knowledge gained from ancient Greece to Western psychology.

Islamic countries stayed abreast of the Western psychology theories and discussed them simultaneously. In these countries, Islamic and Western views of human continued to coexist. Then, Western psychology's interest in Eastern wisdom and spirituality led to more visibility of Islamic psychology studies. Although there are psychologists who do not accept the other psychological approach, today Islamic psychology has emerged and developed as a field that is fed from both sources. Thus, we have made a study area classification that goes from general to specific as psychology – psychology of religion – religious psychology – Islamic psychology – Sufi psychology.

Western psychology seems to shift its attention from the material to the spiritual, and from the negative to the positive sides of the human. Today, behavioral, psychoanalytic, and positive psychology approaches in Western psychology shed light on different aspects of the human being. Islamic psychology also continues to develop a holistic approach to the material, spiritual, and transcendent aspects of human beings and their positive and negative characteristics. Our complementary approach model is functional while utilizing these two sources to understand the human. At first glance, a concept or practice in Western psychology evokes similar concepts and practices from Islamic psychology and vice versa. However, their backgrounds, namely their views of the human, are different from each other. Studying both Western and Islamic psychologies is like having two cell phones, one running iOS and the other Android: although their operating systems are different, they have common applications. So, we offer a three-level complementary approach: (1) comprehending the religious and cultural sources in the wholeness of them; (2) comprehending the psychological sources in the wholeness of them; and (3) utilizing from both by determining the similarities and differences. Hence, we can avoid superficial and selective evaluations that cause us to miss this integrity. In particular, the three-dimensional approach of Islamic psychology to the human nafs is determinant in developing a theory, evaluating a research result, and developing a therapy model in Islamic psychology. Researchers and practitioners of Islamic psychology need to pay attention to this background.

Western psychology today integrates spirituality into psychology when it discovers the capacity of human to transcend her/himself. At the very least, it means that Western psychology accepts the existence of spirituality, that is, an existence that extends beyond physical reality. "Spirituality integrated psychology/psychotherapy" sounds like incorporating a field from non-science into science. Although it does not mention the ontological existence of transcendent being, higher being, or ultimate reality, Western psychology seems to admit the existence of such a transcendent area. The human understanding of Western psychology has evolved from "an intelligent being with a mind (not soul/spirit)" to a bodily being with a spirit. On the other hand, the studies of Islamic psychology are mostly in the form of finding explanations in the Islamic literature of the subjects that are in the scope of psychology today. This approach is not to integrate spirituality into psychology, but to find out the psychological elements within the bio-psycho-spiritual human model of

VIEWS OF WESTERN AND ISLAMIC PSYCHOLOGY OF RELIGION 95

Islam. In Islamic psychology, the human is not a bodily being with a spirit, but a spiritual being with a body.

Since Islamic psychology is a new field in the world agenda, a consensus has not yet been reached on its concepts and practices in the same way as the approaches in Western psychology have emerged and become clear over time. So, Islamic psychology needs some time to be clearer. In this process, we foresee that Islamic psychology will need to put three issues on its agenda.

First, it seems that Islamic psychology will reveal new approaches in itself in the near future. In this book, we have given you an example of the Sufi psychology approach, which is more visible in the literature. However, Islam is a religion spread over a wide geographical area. The Islamic psychology approach is based on the common elements of the Islamic faith. However, as the studies in this field increase over time, differences in Islamic countries will emerge. Thus, different Islamic countries will be able to create subbranches of Islamic psychology based on their own cultural elements and *madhab*s (sects/orders).

Second, until now Islamic psychology literature has mainly focused on the introduction of the Islamic model of the human and psychotherapy applications depending on the Muslim scholars of the past. This accumulation is valuable but also limited to the knowledge of their time. Although the knowledge in the Holy Quran and the Sunnah remains the same, the ideas of scholars developed on the basis of these two sources also contain views that are not compatible with each other or with reality. Islamic psychology needs to adopt a critical approach to its own literature as it does to the Western one, in order not to lead to misconception and misapplications. For example, spiritual well-being and psychological well-being are mixed together in cases where belief in jinn and witchcraft prevents taking psychological support or believing that a psychological disorder such as an eating disorder can be solved by reading the Holy Quran more. Therefore, Islamic psychology needs to face the psychological explanations in Islamic literature.

Third, Islamic psychology often refers to its difference from Western secular psychologies, but it needs a similar explanation for the other side. Since Islamic psychology is at the intersection of psychology, spirituality, and theology it will need to draw clearer boundaries with theology and Tasawwuf in order not to lose the focus of human experience. Otherwise, Islamic psychology and theology and/or Tasawwuf become synonymous. While studying transcendence, which we show as the third dimension in the complementary model, Islamic psychology should focus on its effects on people.

In sum, Islamic psychology is an important area to better understand Muslim clients, but Islamic psychology does not just explain Muslims. These explanations actually contain important determinations about all humanity. With its deep-rooted history and wisdom about life, this approach is the common heritage of humanity. Today, there is an acceptance that the statements of Buddha, Confucius, or Gandhi not only explain their own cultures but also contain determinations about the common attitudes and experiences of humanity. So, this should also apply to Islamic psychology. For this reason, Islamic psychology studies are an important approach to understanding not only Muslims but also human beings in general. What we need is to combine the pertinent findings of Islamic wisdom with scientific thought. Islamic psychology is an important field of study with its historical background, its contribution to the literature today, and its inspiring potential for future studies. When we unlock this potential, we will be one step closer to better understanding ourselves as humanity.

Acknowledgments

There are hidden contributors behind every piece of work. I would like to thank my family, especially my mother and aunt for their prayers. I also appreciate the intellectual and emotional support of colleagues and friends, Assoc. Prof. Kenan Sevinç, Prof. Huriye Martı, Prof. Asiye Şenat, Prof. Ali Köse, Prof. Ali Ayten, Assoc. Prof. Hafize Şule Albayrak, Assoc. Prof. Gülüşan Göcen, Assist. Prof. Ayşe Şentepe, Assist. Prof. Mustafa Derviş Dereli and Sümeyra Güvendi Benzouine.

References

Abu Raiya H. (2013). The Psychology of Islam: Current Empirically Based Knowledge, Potential Changes, and Directions for Future Research. *APA Handbook of Psychology of Religion and Spirituality* (Ed. K. Pargament). Washington: APA.

Abu Raiya H. (2014). Western Psychology and Muslim Psychology in Dialogue: Comparisons Between a Quranic Theory of Personality and Freud's and Jung's Ideas. *J Relig Health*, 53, 326–338.

Abu Raiya, H. & Pargament, K.I. (2010). Religiously Integrated Psychotherapy with Muslim Clients: From Research to Practice. *Professional Psychology: Research and Practice*, 41 (2), 181–188.

Adam, C. (1963). *Descartes Hayatı ve Eserleri* [Life and Publications of Descartes] (Trans. M. Karasan). Ankara: MEB.

Ağılkaya-Şahin, Z. (2015). The Problem of Appropriate Psychology of Religion Measures for Non-Western-Christian Samples with Respect to the Turkish-Islamic Religious

VIEWS OF WESTERN AND ISLAMIC PSYCHOLOGY OF RELIGION   97

Landscape. *Psychology of Religion in Turkey* (Eds. Z. Ağılkaya, A. Ayten, H. Streib & R.W. Hood). Leiden: Brill.

Ahmed, S. & Amer, M.M. (Eds.). (2012). *Counseling Muslims: Handbook of Mental Health Issues and Interventions.* New York & London: Routledge.

Akün, Ö.F. (1998). Hoca Tahsin [Hodja Tahsin]. *Türkiye Diyanet Vakfı İslam Ansiklopedisi,* v. 18. Ankara: TDV, 198–206.

Ali, Ahmed (1993). *Al-Qur'an: A Contemporary Translation.* Princeton, NJ: Princeton University Press.

Altınlı-Macic M. & Coleman, T. (2015). Spirituality and Religion: An Emprical Study Using a Turkish Muslim Sample. *Psychology of Religion in Turkey* (Eds. Z. Ağılkaya, A. Ayten, H. Streib & R. Hood). Leiden: Brill.

Ames, E.S. (1919). Review of Jesus, the Christ, in the Light of Psychology [Review of the book *Jesus, the Christ, in the Light of Psychology*, by G.S. Hall]. *Psychological Bulletin,* 16 (8), 295–298.

Anbari, M.; Baranovich, D.L. & Zailaini, M.A. (2019). History of Psychology in Islamic Republic of Iran. *International Journal of Recent Technology and Engineering (IJRT),* 8 (32), 786–790.

Arasteh, A.R. & Sheikh, E.A. (2010). Tasavvuf: Evrensel Benliğe Giden Yol [Tasawwuf: The Way to the Universal Self]. In *Sufi Psikolojisi* [Sufi Psychology] (Ed. K. Sayar). İstanbul: Timaş.

Arıcan, K.M. (2006). Din, Psikoloji ve Felsefe: Mustafa Şekip Tunç'ta Din Felsefesi Din Psikolojisi İlişkisi [Religion, Psychology and Philosophy: The Relationship Between Psychology of Religion and Philosopy of Religion in Mustafa Şekip Tunç]. *EKEV Akademi Dergisi,* 10 (28), 127–142.

Armaner, N. (1973). *Psikopatolojide Dini Belirtiler* [Religious Symptoms in Psychopathology]. Ankara: Demirbaş Yayınları.

Asante, K.O. (2012). Psychology in Ghana: Origin, Prospects and Challenges. In History of Psychology. *International Journal of Psychology,* 47 (1), 459–466.

Ayhan, H. (2000). İlahiyat Fakültesi [Faculty of Theology]. *Türkiye Diyanet Vakfı İslam Ansiklopedisi,* v. 22. Ankara: TDV, 70–72.

Ayten, A. (2018). *Din ve Sağlık* [Religion and Health], İstanbul: Marmara Akademi.

Ayten, A. (2021). *Doğa Bize Emanet.* [Nature Is Entrusted to Us]. İstanbul: İz.

Ayten, A. & Düzgüner, S. (2017). *Tasavvuf Psikolojisi* [Psychology of Tasawwuf]. İstanbul: Sufi Kitap.

Ayten, A. & Hussain, A.M. (2021). *Psychology and Islam.* İstanbul: İFAV.

Ayten, A.; Göcen, G.; Sevinç, K. & Öztürk, E.E. (2012). Dini Başa Çıkma, Şükür ve Hayat Memnuniyeti İlişkisi [The Relationships Among Religious Coping, Gratitude and Life Satisfaction]. *Din Bilimleri Akademik Araştırma Dergisi,* 12 (2), 45–79.

Babaoğlu, A. (2002). *Psikiyatri Tarihi* [History of Psychiatry]. İstanbul: Okuyan Us.

Badri, M.B. (1979). *The Dilemma of Muslim Psychologists.* London: MWH London.

Balhi, A.Z. (2022). *Beden ve Ruh Sağlığı: Korunma Yolları ve Tavsiyeler (Masalih'al-abdan wa'l-anfus)* [Physical and Mental Health: Prevention Ways and Recommendations], (Trans. M. Uysal). İstanbul: Endülüs.

Barnard, G.W. (2000). Diving into the Depths: Reflections on Psychology as a Religion. In *Religion and Psychology: Mapping the Terrain Contemporary Dialogues, Future Prospects* (Eds. D. Jonte-Pace & W.B. Parsons). London & New York: Routledge.

Batur, S. (2003). Türkiye'de Psikoloji Tarihi Yazımı Üzerine [On Psychology the Writing of Historiography in Turkey]. *Toplum ve Bilim*, 98, 255–264.

Belen, F.Z. (2019). Osmanlı'da Psikolojik Sağlık Uygulamaları ve Osmanlıca Psikoloji Literatürü Üzerine Bir Değerlendirme [An Evaluation on Psychological Health Practices in The Ottoman Empire and Ottoman Psychology Literature]. *Kalemname*, 4 (7), 65–78.

Bellaj, T. (2012). Culture and Neuropsychological Assessment: Issues Discussed from The Tunisian Experience. In History of Psychology. *International Journal of Psychology*, 47 (1), 459–466.

Belzen, J.A. (2005). A Way Out of the Crisis? From Völkerpsychologie to Cultural Psychology of Religion. *Theory & Psychology*, 15 (6), 812–838.

Benjafield, J.G. (1996). *A History of Psychology*. Needham Heights: Allyn & Bacon.

Benjamin, L.T. (2019). *Modern Psikolojinin Kısa Bir Tarihi* [A Brief History of Modern Psychology] (Trans. C. Malakcıoğlu). Ankara: Nobel Yaşam.

Benli, Z. (2017). Hacamat Tedavisi [Cupping (Hajamat)]. *Uluslararası Sosyal Bilimler Dergisi*, 1 (6), 46–53.

Bidwell, D.R. (1999). Ken Wilber's Transpersonal Psychology: An Introduction and Preliminary Critique. *Pastoral Psychology*, 48 (2), 81–90.

Bilgin N. (1988). *Başlangıçtan Günümüze Türk Psikoloji Bibliyografyası* [Turkish Psychology Bibliography from The Beginning to the Present]. İzmir: Ege Üniversitesi Edebiyat Fakültesi.

Brock, A.; Mueller, C.; Schrott, R.; Kappelhoff, H.; Mar, R. & Goldberg, A. (2012). Towards A History of The Indigenisation Movement in Psychology. In History of Psychology. *International Journal of Psychology*, 47 (1), 459–466.

Bruno, F. (1996). *Psikoloji Tarihi* [History of Psychology] (Trans. G. Sevdiren). İstanbul: Kibele.

Çakan, İ.L. (2016). *Hadis Usulü* [Hadith Methodology]. İstanbul: İFAV.

Çetin, İ. (1994). John Locke'da Ahlak Kurallarının Kaynağı [The Source of Ethics in John Locke]. *Uludağ Üniversitesi İlahiyat Fakültesi Dergisi*, 6 (6), 167–176.

Crapps, R. (1986). *An Introduction to Psychology of Religion*. Macon, GA: Mercer University Press.

Descartes, R. (1983). *Felsefenin İlkeleri* [Principles of Philosophy] (Trans. M. Akın). İstanbul: Say.

Diyanet İşleri Başkanlığı [Presidency of Religious Affairs (in Turkish Republic)] (2020). *Hadislerle İslam* [Islam Through Hadiths]. Ankara: Diyanet İşleri Başkanlığı.

Dündar, M.; Emekli, R. & Şener, E. (2019). Anadolu'daki Tıbbın Doğuşu, Dünyadaki İlk Tıp Okulu Olarak Gevher Nesibe Tıp Medresesi ve Darüşşifası [The Birth of Medicine in Anatolia, The First Medical School Worldwide: Gevher Nesibe Madrasah]. *Bilimname*, 39 (3), 79–103.

Durusoy, A. (1999). İbn Sina Felsefesi [Philosophy of Ibn Sina]. *Türkiye Diyanet Vakfı İslam Ansiklopedisi*, v. 20. Ankara: TDV, 322–331.

Düzgüner, S. (2007). Mevlevî Sema Ayini'nin İnsan Psikolojisine Etkileri Üzerine Bir Araştırma [A Research on the Influence of Mawlawi Sema Ritual on Human Psychology]. *Marife*, 7 (3), 195–214.

Düzgüner, S. (2013a). Ruh-Beden ve İnsan-Aşkın Varlık İlişkisine Yönelik Psikolojik Yaklaşımın Tarihi Serüveni [The Historical Process of Psychological Approach to the Relationship Between Body and Soul and Human and Transcendent Being]. *Marmara Üniversitesi İlahiyat Fakültesi Dergisi*, 45 (2), 253–284.

Düzgüner, S. (2013b). The Intersection Point of Mysticism, Spirituality, and Religiosity: An Empirical Study on Mawlawi Sema Ritual. Paper presented at *the 2013 Congress of the International Association for the Psychology of Religion*, Lausanne, Switzerland.

Düzgüner, S. (2017). Dini Psikoloji ve İslam Psikolojisi Bağlamında Din Psikolojisini Yeniden Düşünmek [Reconsidering Psychology of Religion in the Context of Religious Psychology and Islamic Psychology]. *İslami İlimler Dergisi Din Psikolojisi Özel Sayısı*, 12 (3), 133–164.

Düzgüner, S. (2021). *Maneviyat Algısı ve Yansımaları (Türkiye-Amerika Karşılaştırması)*, [Perception of Spirituality and Its Reflections (Comparison Between Türkiye and the U.S.)]. İstanbul: Çamlıca.

Düzgüner, S. & Ayten, A. (2020). *Manevi Danışmanlık ve Rehberlik Hizmetleri Temel Bilgiler* [Rudiments for Spiritual Counseling and Guidance Services] (Ed. S. Düzgüner ve A. Ayten). Ankara: Diyanet İşleri Başkanlığı.

Düzgüner, S. & Şentepe, A. (2015). Characteristic Themes in Psychology of Religion in Turkey: Muslim Thinkers' Views About Human Psychology and Psychology of Sufism. In *Psychology of Religion in Turkey* (Eds. Z. Ağılkaya-Şahin, H. Streib, A. Ayten & R.W. Hood). Leiden & Boston: Brill.

Egemen, B.Z. (1952). *Din Psikolojisi* [Psychology of Religion]. Ankara: Türk Tarih Kurumu Basımevi.

Emerson, J.G. (2000). Pastoral Psychology in the Dynamic of the New Millennium, *Pastoral Psychology*, 48 (4), 251–291.

Erdem, H. (1999). *Bazı Felsefe Meseleleri* [Some Philosopy Issues]. Konya: Hü-Er.

Erdem, H. (2000). *İlkçağ Felsefesi Tarihi* [History of Ancient Philosophy]. Konya: Hü-Er.

Erdem, Ö.F. (2013). William James'in Gifford Konferansları ve The Varieties of Religious Experience İsimli Eserinin Yankıları Üzerine Bir Analiz [The Analysis of The Reflections of William James' Gifford Lectures and his Book "The Varieties of Religious Experience"]. *Marife*, 13 (1), 127–138.

Erenay-Uyaver, A.; Karatepe, H.T. & Tabo, A. (2015). Correlation of The Disease Symptoms of Obsessive-Compulsive Disordered Patients with Their Religious Attitude and Behaviours. In *Psychology of Religion in Turkey* (Eds. Z. Ağılkaya-Şahin, H. Streib, A. Ayten & R.W. Hood). Leiden & Boston: Brill.

Erer, S. & Atıcı, E. (2010). Selçuklu ve Osmanlılarda Müzikle Tedavi Yapılan Hastaneler [Hospitals Using Music Therapy in Seljuks and Ottoman]. *Uludağ Üniversitesi Tıp Fakültesi Dergisi*, 36 (1), 29–32.

Ertürk, E.M. (2017). Seküler Dünyada Yeni Bir Yaşam Tarzı Olarak Maneviyat Tebliğine Müzakere 1 [Disscussion 1 on the Paper "Spirituality as a New Lifestyle in a Secular World"]. In Sekülerleşme ve Din [Secularization and Religion]. Ankara: A Kitap.

Fancher, R.E. (1997). *Ruhbilimin Öncüleri* [Pioneers of Psychology] (Trans. A. Yardımlı). İstanbul: İdea.

Farabi, E.M. (1997). *İdeal Devlet/al-Madinah al-Fadila* [The Virtuous City] (Trans. A. Arslan). Ankara: Vadi.

Frager, R. (2005). *Kalp, Nefs & Ruh: Sufi Psikolojisinde Gelişim, Denge ve Uyum.* [Heart, Self & Soul: Development, Balance and Harmony in Sufi Psychology] (Trans. İ. Kapaklıkaya). İstanbul: Gelenek.

Freud, S. (1998). *Hz. Musa ve Tektanrıcılık* [Moses and Monotheism] (Trans. K. Şipal). İstanbul: Cem.

Freud, S. (2004). *Psikanaliz Üzerine* [On Psychoanalysis] (Trans. A.A. Öneş). İstanbul: Say.

Freud, S. (2006a). *Dinin Kökenleri/Totem ve Tabu* [The Origins of Religion/Totem and Taboo] (Trans. S. Budak). İstanbul: Öteki.

Freud, S. (2006b). *Uygarlık, Din ve Toplum/Bir Yanılsamanın Geleceği* [Civilization, Religion, and Society/The Future of an Illusion] (Trans. S. Budak). İstanbul: Öteki.

Freud, S. (2006c). *Dinin Kökenleri/Saplantılı Eylemler ve Dinî Uygulamalar* [The Origins of Religion/Obsessive Acts and Religious Practices] (Trans. S. Budak). İstanbul: Öteki.

Ghazali, A.H. (1992). *İhya-u Ulumu'd-Din* [The Revival of Religious Sciences] (Trans. A. Serdaroğlu). İstanbul: Bedir.

Gilovich, T., & Medvec, V.H. (1995). The Experience of Regret: What, When and Why. *Psychological Review*, 102, 379–395.

Göcen, G. (2012). *Şükür: Pozitif Psikolojiden Din Psikolojisine Köprü* [Gratitude: A Bridge from Positive Psychology to the Psychology of Religion]. İstanbul: DEM.

Göcen, G. (2013). Pozitif Psikoloji Düzleminde Psikolojik İyi Olma ve Dini Yönelim İlişkisi: Yetişkinler Üzerine Bir Araştırma [Psychological Well Being and Religious Orientation in Terms of Positive Psychology: A Research About Adult]. *Toplum Bilimleri Dergisi*, 7 (13), 97–130.

Göcen, G. (2016). Kadirşinaslık ve Öznel İyi Oluş Suça Sürüklenen Çocuklar Üzerine Nicel Bir Araştırma [Appreciation and Subjective Well Being: A Quantitative Research on Juvenile Driven into Delinquency]. *İnsan ve Toplum Bilimleri Araştırmaları Dergisi*, 5 (4), 966–990.

Gökberk, M. (1993). *Felsefe Tarihi* [History of Philosophy]. İstanbul: Remzi.

Gözütok, T.T. (2013). *Rifat Bin Mehmed Emin'in İlm-İ Ahval-İ Ruh ve Usul-İ Tefekkür Adlı Eserinin Türk Psikoloji Tarihi'ndeki Yeri* [The Role of the Book Ilmi Ahvali Ruh ve Usuli Tefekkür by Rıfat bin Mehmet Emin in the History of Turkish Psychology]. Unpublished Master Thesis, Ankara University, Institute of Social Sciences, Department of Philosophy (History of Science). Ankara.

Guénon, R. (1989). *İslam Maneviyatı ve Taoculuğa Toplu Bakış* [Overview of Islamic Spirituality and Taoism] (Trans. M. Kanık). İstanbul: İnsan.

Gümüşsoy, M.B. (2018). Kindi'nin Ahlak Felsefesi ve Modern Bilişsel Terapide Üzüntü, Depresyon ve Çözüm Teknikleri [Sadness, Depression and Therapy Techniques in Kindi's Moral Philosophy and Modern Cognitive Psychology]. *Türkiye Bütüncül Psikoterapi Dergisi*, 1 (2), 121–133.

Güngörmüş-Kona, G. (2005). *Batıda Aydınlanma Doğuda Batılılaşma* [Enlightment in The West, Westernization in The East]. İstanbul: Okumuş Adam.

Gürses, İ. (2019). *Sufi Kişilik Psikolojisi: Melamiler Örneği* [Sufi Psychology of Personality: The Case of Malamis]. Ankara: Hece.

Gürsu, O. (2016). İslam Düşünürü Belhi'nin (849–934) Ruh Sağlığına Yönelik Görüşlerinin Modern Psikoloji Doğrultusunda Değerlendirilmesi [An Evaluation of The Views of Islamic Thinker Al-Balkhi (849–934) within The Context of Modern Psychology]. *Dokuz Eylül Üniversitesi İlahiyat Fakültesi Dergisi*, Din Psikolojisi Özel Sayısı, 271–309.

Güven, M. & Güven, İ.F. (2021). *Türkiye'de Din Psikolojisinin Son 20 Yılı* [Last 20 Years of Psychology of Religion in Turkey]. İstanbul: DEM.

Hamdan, A. (2007). A Case Study of a Muslim Client: Incorporating Religious Beliefs and Practices. *Journal of Multicultural Counseling and Development*, 35, 92–100.

Haque, A. (1998). Psychology and Religion: Their Relationship and Integration from an Islamic Perspective. *The American Journal of Islamic Social Sciences*, 15 (4), 97–116.

Haque, A. (2004). Psychology from Islamic Perspective: Contributions of Early Muslim Scholars and Challenges to Contemporary Muslim Psychologists. *Journal of Religion and Health*, 43 (4), 357–377.

Haque, A.; Khan, F.; Keshavarzi, H. & Rothman, A. (2016). Integrating Islamic Traditions in Modern Psychology: Research Trends in Last Ten Years. *Journal of Muslim Mental Health*, 10 (1), 75–100.

Hatunoğlu, A. (2014). Türk İslam Hekimlerinin Psikoloji Biliminin Gelişimine Katkıları ve Psikolojik Hastalıklara Tedavi Yöntemleri [Turkish Islamic Contrubutions to the Development of The Psychology of Doctors and Psychological Disorders Treatment]. *Akademik Sosyal Araştırmalar Dergisi*, 2 (5), 255–263.

Helliwell, J.F.; Richard-Layard, R.; Sachs, J.D.; De Neve, J.; Aknin, L.B. & Wang, S. (2021). *World Happiness Report*, https://worldhappiness.report/ed/2021/, 19.11.2021.

Hızlı, M. (1987). Kuruluşundan Osmanlılara Kadar Medreseler [The Madrasah from Its Establishment to The Ottomans]. *Uludağ Üniversitesi İlahiyat Fakültesi Dergisi* 2 (2), 273–281.

Hökeleki, H. (2016). Türkiye'de Din, Dindarlık ve Din Psikolojisi Araştırmaları: Psikolojide Yerellik ve Evrensellik Tartışmaları Bağlamında Bir Değerlendirme, [Researches of Religion, Religiosity And Psychology of Religion In Turkey: An Assessment In The Context of Discussions of Locality And Universality In Psychology]. *Dokuz Eylül Üniversitesi İlahiyat Fakültesi Dergisi*, Special Issue on Psychology of Religion, 311–333.

Hökelekli, H. (2005). *Din Psikolojisi* [Psychology of Religion]. Ankara: TDV.

Hökelekli, H. (2010). *İslam Psikolojisi Yazıları* [Islamic Psychology Writings]. İstanbul: DEM.

Hood, R.W. & Spilka, B. (2012). A Chorological Overview of The Psychology of Religion. *Religious Studies and Theology*, 31 (2), 129–146.

Hood, R.W.; Hill, P.C. & Williamson, W.P. (2005). *The Psychology of Religious Fundamentalism: An Intratextual Model*. New York: Guilford Press.

Horozcu, Ü. (2010). Darülfünun İlahiyat Fakültesindeki Psikoloji Çalışmaları: Mustafa Şekip Tunç Örnegi [Psychology Studies at Darulfunun Faculty of Theology: The Example of Mustafa Şekip Tunç]. *Darulfünun İlahiyat Sempozyumu*. İstanbul, 399–403.

Hosseingholizadeh, M. (2013). *Türkiye'de ve İran'da Modern Psikolojinin Başlangıcı Hoca Tahsin Efendi & Dr. Siyasi* [The Introduction of Modern Psychology in Iran and Turkey: Hodja Tahsin & Dr. Siyasi]. Unpublished Master Thesis, Ankara University, Institute of Social Sciences, Department of Philosophy (History of Science). Ankara.

Hothersall, D. (1984). *History of Psychology*. Philadelphia: Temple University Press.

Hujwiri, A.J. (2014). *Keşfu'l Mahcûb* [Kashf al- Mahjuub/Revelation of the Veiled] (Trans. S. Uludağ). İstanbul: Dergah.

Hunsinger, D.D. (1995). *Theology and Pastoral Counseling: A New Interdisciplinary Approach*. Michigan: William B. Eerdmans Publishing Company.

Ibn Rushd, M. (2007). *Telhîsü Kitabi'n-Nefs* [Telhisu Kitabin Nefs/Psychology Commentary] (Trans. A. Arkan). İstanbul: Litera.

Ibrahim, A. (2013). Arab World Psychology. *The Encyclopedia of Cross-Cultural Psychology* (Ed. D.K. Kenneth), v. 1. New York: John Wiley.

Igarashi, Y. (2012). History of Japanese Psychology as a Local History: Americanisation and Psychologisation. In History of Psychology. *International Journal of Psychology*, 47 (1), 459–466.

İhsanoğlu, E. (1993). Dârü'l-Fünun [Dar'ul-Funun]. *Türkiye Diyanet Vakfı İslam Ansiklopedisi*, v. 8. Ankara: TDV, 521–525.

Iqbal, N. & Skinner, R. (2021). Islamic Psychology: Emergence and Current Challenges. *Archive for the Psychology of Religion*, 43 (1), 65–77.

James, W. (1961). *The Varieties of Religious Experience*. New York: New American Library.

Johnson, E.L. & Jones, S.L. (2000). A History of Christians in Psychology. *Psychology and Chiristianity* (Ed. E.L. Johnson & S.L. Jones). Westmont: Inter Varsity Press.

Jung, C.G. (1998). *Psikoloji ve Din* [Psychology and Religion] (Trans. R. Karabey). İstanbul: Okyanus.

Kahya, E. (1998). Hipokrat [Hippocrates]. *Türkiye Diyanet Vakfı İslam Ansiklopedisi*, v. 18. Ankara: TDV, 119–121.

Karaca, F. (2011). *Din Psikolojisi* [Psychology of Religion]. Trabzon: Eser Ofset.

Karagöz, S. (2020). Manevi İçerikli Grup Rehberliğinin Özel Gereksinimli Çocuk Sahibi Annelerin Dini Başa Çıkma Düzeylerine Etkisinin İncelenmesi [Analysis of the Effect of Group Guidance with Spiritual Content on the Religious Coping Levels of Mothers of Children with Special Needs]. *Dergiabant*, 8 (1), 298–317.

Kavaklı, A. (2010). Akupunktur [Acapuncture]. *Fırat Tıp Dergisi*, 15 (1), 1–4.

Kaya, M. (2007). Ebu Bekir Razi [Abu Bakr Al-Razı/Rhazes]. *Türkiye Diyanet Vakfı İslam Ansiklopedisi*, v. 34. Ankara: TDV, 479–485.

Kayıklık, H. (2011a). *Din Psikolojisi: Bireysel Dindarlık Üzerine* [Psycholgy of Religion: On Individual Religiosity]. Adana: Karahan.

Kayıklık, H. (2011b). *Tasavvuf Psikolojisi* [The Psychology of Tasawwuf]. Ankara: Akçağ.

Kemal, Y. (1878). *Gâyetü'l-Beyan fi Hakikati'l-İnsan yahut İlm-i Ahvâl-i Ruh* [An Attempt to Express the Essence of Human Being or The States of Soul/Spirit]. İstanbul: Mihran Matbaası.

Keshavarzi, H.; Khan, F; Ali, B. & Awaad, R. (Eds.) (2021). *Applying Islamic Principles to Clinical Mental Health Care: Introducing Traditional Islamically Integrated Psychotherapy*. New York & London: Routledge.

Khodayarifard, M.; Azarbaijani M.; Shahabi, R. & Zandi, S. (2021). *Introduction to Islamic Psychology*. Leiden: Brill.

Kindi, Y.İ. (1998). *Üzüntüden Kurtulma Yolları/Al-Hila li-Daf'i'l-Ahzan* [The Art of Disepelling Sorrows] (Trans. M. Çağrıcı). İstanbul: İFAV.

Kılıç, R. (2015). Türkiye'de Modern Psikolojinin Tarihi: İlm-İ Ahvâl-İ Ruh/İlmü'n-Nefs/Ruhiyyat [History of Modern Psychology in Turkey: Ilm-i Ahwal-i Ruh/Ilmu'n-Nafs/Ruhiyyat]. *Kebikeç*, 40, 21–36.

Koenig, H. (2016). The Framework of Religious-Spiritual Counselling: Religion, Spirituality, And Health: Research, Clinical Applications, and Resources. In *Religious-Spiritual Counselling & Care* (Eds. A. Ayten, M. Koç, N. Tınaz & M.A. Doğan). İstanbul: DEM.

Koenig, H.; Mccullough, M. & Larson, D.B. (2001). *Handbook of Religion and Health: A Century of Research Reviewed.* New York: Oxford University Press.

Korkman, H. (2017). Ortaçağ İslam Felsefesinde Psikoloji İle İlgili Görüşler [Ideas About Psychology in Medievel Islamic Philosophy]. *Asya Öğretim Dergisi* [*Asian Journal of Instruction*]. 5 (1), 12–27.

Köse, A. (2006). Psikoloji ve Din: Bir Dargın Bir Barışık Kardeşler [Psychology and Religion: On Again Off Again Sisters/Brothers]. *İslamî Araştırmalar Dergisi, Din Psikolojisi Özel Sayısı*, 19 (3), 1–11.

Köse, A. & Ayten, A. (2012). *Din Psikolojisi* [Psychology of Religion]. İstanbul: Timaş.

Küçük, H. (2011). *Tasavvufa Giriş* [Introduction to Tasawwuf]. İstanbul: DEM.

Küçük, O.N. (2009). *Mevlana'ya Göre Manevi Gelişim* [Spiritual Development According to Mawlana]. İstanbul: İnsan.

Kurtça, H. (2020). *15–19. Yüzyıllar Arasında Osmanlı'da ve İngiltere'de Akıl Hastalarına Tedavi Sunan İki Hastanenin Karşılaştırılması: Edirne Sultan II. Bayezid Darüşşifası ve Londra Bethlem Hastanesi* [Comparing the Treatment Provided to the Mentally Ill in Two Hospitals from the Ottoman Empire and Britain during the 15th–19th Centuries: Edirne Sultan Bayezid II Dar al-Shifa' and London Bethlem Hospital]. Unpublished Master Thesis, Marmara University, Institute of Social Sciences, Department of Psychology of Religion, İstanbul.

Kurtuluş, M. (2016). Osmanlı'nın Meczûbları ve Mecnûnları: Erken Modern Dönemde Hastaneler ve Deliliğe Bakış [Ottoman Majzubs and Majnuns: A Glance into The Ottoman Hospitals and Madness in the Early Modern Period]. *Millî Folklor*, 112, 100–113.

Liangyue, D. (2001). Chinese Acupuncture-Moxibustion. In *Traditional Medicine in Asia* (Ed. R.R. Chaudhury & U.M. Rafei). New Delhi: World Health Organization Regional Office for South-East Asia.

Locke, J. (1992). Bize Verilmiş Bir Ahlak Kuralı Ya Da Tabiat Kanunu Var Mıdır? Evet [Is There a Moral Rule or Natural Law Given to Us? Yes]. *Uludağ Üniversitesi İlahiyat Fakültesi Dergisi* (Trans. İ. Çetin). 4 (4), 333–338.

Loewenthal, K. (2017). *Din Psikolojisi* [Psychology of Religion] (Trans. M. Ulu). Kayseri: Kimlik.

Maslow, A. (1996). *Dinler Değerler Doruk Deneyimler* [Religions, Values and Peak Experiences] (Trans. H.K. Sönmez). İstanbul: Kuraldışı.

Maslow, A. (2001). *İnsan Olmanın Psikolojisi* [Toward a Psychology of Being] (Trans. O. Gündüz). İstanbul: Kuraldışı.

McKinney, F. (1960). Psychology in Turkey: Speculation Concerning Psychology's Growth and Area Cultures. *The American Psychologist*, 15 (11), 717–721.

Mebarki, B. (2012). Promoting Psychology in Algeria: Difficulties of a Culturally-embedded Discipline. In History of Psychology. *International Journal of Psychology*, 47 (1), 459–466.

VIEWS OF WESTERN AND ISLAMIC PSYCHOLOGY OF RELIGION   105

Merriam-Webster (2021). Psyche. https://www.merriam-webster.com/dictionary/psyche
.23.11.2021.

Merter, M. (2014). *Nefs Psikolojisi* [Psychology of Nafs]. İstanbul: Kaknüs.

Mohamed, W. (2012). Psychology in Egypt: Challenges and Hopes. *Psychology International*, 23 (1), Https://Www.Apa.Org/İnternational/Pi/2012/03/Egypt, 03.08.2021.

Muhasibi, H. (1998). *er-Riâye*, [ar-Riayah] (Trans. H. Küçük & Ş. Filiz). İstanbul: İnsan.

Muhasibi, H. (2009). *Nefsin Terbiyesi/Muatabah an-Nafs* [Disciplining the Nafs/Self] (Trans. M.Z. Tiryaki). İstanbul: Hayykitap.

Muti, İ. (2002). Uygurların İslam'ı Kabul Ettikleri İlk Dönemlerdeki İslam Medreseleri [Islamic Madrasah in the Early Periods of Uyghur Conversion to Islam]. *Divan*, 1, 299–311.

Nicholson, R. (1950). *Rumi: Poet and Mystic*, London: George Allen and Unwin.

Özbaydar, B. (1970). *Din ve Tanrı İnancının Gelişmesi Üzerine Bir Araştırma* [A Study of Development of Belief in Religion and God]. İstanbul: Baha Matbaası.

Özdemir, N. & Düzgüner, S. (2020). Psikolojik Açıdan Suçluluk, Pişmanlık ve Günahkarlığın Kapsamı ve Yakın Kavramlar Arasındaki Yeri [The Scope of Guilty, Regret and Sinfulness from Psychological Perspective and Their Place Among Close Concepts]. *Ondokuz Mayıs Üniversitesi İlahiyat Fakültesi Dergisi*, 49, 497–529.

Özkaya, Ş.Y. (2016). Osmanlı'nın Tıp Anlayışını ve Akıl Hastalarına Yaklaşımını Belirleyen Faktörler ile Bu Anlayışın "Mâ-Hazar"da Tezâhürü [The Factors Determining Ottoman Approach to Medicine and Approach to Mentally Ills and the Manifestation of This Understanding "Ma Hazar"]. In *v. Türkiye Lisansüstü Çalışmalar Kongresi Bildiriler Kitabı-II*, Isparta.

Pazarlı, O. (1968). *Din Psikolojisi* [Psychology of Religion]. İstanbul: Remzi.

Peker, H. (2012). *Din Psikolojisi* [Psychology of Religion]. İstanbul: Çamlıca.

PEW (2012). *The World's Muslims: Unity and Diversity.* https://www.pewforum.org/2012 /08/09/the-worlds-muslims-unity-and-diversity-executive-summary/, 19.11.2021.

Rahnama, M.; Khoshknab, M.F.; Maddah, S.S. & Ahmadi, F. (2012). Iranian Cancer Patients' Perception of Spirtuality: A Qualitative Content Analysis Study. *BMC Nursing*, 11, 11–19.

Razi, F. (2018). *Et-Tıbbu'r-Rûhanî: Ruh Sağlığı* [Et-Tibbu'r Ruhani: Mental/Spiritual Health] (Trans. H. Karaman). İstanbul: İz.

Reuder, M.E. (1999). A History of Division 36, www.apadivisions.org>about>history, 28.07.2017.

Reyes, A. & Moreno, A.V. (2012). Psychology in Cuba: Past and Present. In History of Psychology. *International Journal of Psychology*, 47 (1), 459–466.

Reza, F.G. (2010). A Glance on "Nafs" and "Mind" and Their Roles in Understanding. *Marifat-i Falsafi*, 7 (2), 41–70.

Robinson, D. (1995). *An Intellectual History of Psychology.* London: The University of Wisconsin.

Rothman, A. & Coyle, A. (2018). Toward a Framework for Islamic Psychology and Psychotherapy: An Islamic Model of the Soul. *Journal of Religion and Health*, 57, 1731–1744.

Sayar, K. (2010). Geçmişin Bilgeliği Bugünün Psikoterapileriyle Buluşabilir mi? Sufi Psikolojisi Örneği [Can the Wisdom of the Past Meet the Psychotherapies of Today? A Case of Sufi Psychologly]. In *Sufi Psikolojisi* [Sufi Psychology] (Ed. K. Sayar). İstanbul: Timaş.

Schultz, D. & Schultz, S.E. (2002). *Modern Psikoloji Tarihi* [A History of Modern Psychology] (Trans. Y. Aslay). İstanbul: Kaknüs.

Şeker, N. (2013). Hz. Peygamber'in Hadislerinde Koruyucu Hekimlik: Hacamat Örneği [Prophet and Preventive Medicine: The Case of Bloodletting]. *Kahramanmaraş Sütçü İmam Üniversitesi İlahiyat Fakültesi Dergisi*, 21, 156–188.

Şentürk, H. (2008). *İbadet Psikolojisi: Hz. Peygamber Örneği* [Worship Psychology: Example of Prophet Muhammad]. İstanbul: İz.

Sevinç, K. (2013). Türkiye'de Din Psikolojisi Alanında Yapılan Lisansüstü Tezler Üzerine Bir İnceleme [A Study on the Graduate Theses of the Field of the Psychology of Religion in Turkey]. *Sakarya Üniversitesi İlahiyat Fakültesi Dergisi*, 28 (2), 243–269.

Sevinç, K.; Coleman, T. & Hood, R.W. (2018). Non-Belief: An Islamic Perspective. *Secularism and Nonreligion*, 7 (5), 1–12.

Shani, Y.; Danziger, S. & Zeelenberg, M. (2015). Choosing Between Options Associated with Past and Future Regret. *Organizational Behavior and Human Decision Processes*, 126, 107–114.

Skinner, B.F. (1972). *Beyond Freedom and Dignity*. New York & Kanada: A Bantam/ Vintage Book.

Söylev, Ö.F. (2014). Psikolojik Sağlık Hakkında İslam Tıp Tarihinin İlk Örneklerinden Mesalih'ul-Ebdan ve'l-Enfüs [One of the First Examples of Islamic History of Medicine on Psychological Health: Mesalihu'l Ebdan ve'l Enfus]. *İslam Medeniyeti Araştırmaları Dergisi*, 1 (1), 196–202.

Tarhan, N. (2013). *Mesnevi Terapi* [The Mathnawi Therapy]. İstanbul: Timaş.

Taylan, N. (2006). *İslam Felsefesi* [Philosophy of Islam]. İstanbul: Ensar Neşriyat.

Tevfik, M. (1975). *Ruhi Bunalımlar ve İslam Ruhiyatı* [Psychologcial/Spiritual Crisis and Islamic Spirituality]. İstanbul: Bedir.

Toğrol, B. (1987). Türkiye'de Psikolojinin Tarihçesi [History of Psychology in Turkey]. *Tecrübi Psikoloji Çalışmaları*, 15, 8–10.

Topçu, N. (2005). *İslam ve İnsan, Mevlana ve Tasavvuf* [Islam and Human, Mawlana and Tasawwuf]. İstanbul: Dergah.

Toshihiko & Toyo Izutsu (1981). *The Theory of Beauty in the Classical Aesthetics of Japan*. The Hague, Boston & London: Martinus Nijhoff.

Tunaboylu-İkiz, T. (1999). Türk Psikiyatri Tarihi ve Psikanalizin Yeri [Turkish Psychiatry History and Place of Psychoanalysis]. *Psikoloji Çalışmaları*, 21, 159–168.

Ülken, H.Z. (1924a). Anadolu Tarihinde Dini Ruhiyyat Müşahedeleri: Burak Baba, Geyikli Baba [Religious Spirituality/Psychology Observations in Anatolian History: Burak Baba, Geyikli Baba]. *Mihrab*, 13–14, 434–448.

Ülken, H.Z. (1924b). Anadolu Tarihinde Dini Ruhiyyat Müşahedeleri: Hacı Bektaş-ı Veli [Religious Spirituality/Psychology Observations in Anatolian History: Haji Baktash Wali]. *Mihrab*, 15–16, 515–530.

Ülken, H.Z. (1946). *Tasavvuf Psikolojisi* [The Psychology of Tasawwuf]. İstanbul: Kenan.

Ulusoy, T.İ. (1970). *Din Psikolojisi* [Psychology of Religion]. İstanbul: Hisar.

Utz, A. (2011). *Psychology from the Islamic Perspective*. Riyadh, Saudi Arabia: International Islamic Publishing House.

Uysal, S. (2021). *Gelenek ile Gelecek Arasında İslami Psikoloji* [Islamic Psychology Between Tradition and Future]. İstanbul: Çamlıca.

Vandenbos, G.R. (Ed.) (2015). *APA Dictionary of Psychology*. Washington: APA.

Varlı, N. (2019). Erken Dönem İslâm Âlimlerinin Psikolojiye Katkıları: Akıl, Nefs, Ruh Kavramları [The Controbution of Early Islamic Scholars to Psychology: The Concepts of Aql, Nafs, and Ruh]. *Antakiyat: Hatay Mustafa Kemal Üniversitesi İlahiyat Fakültesi Dergisi*, 2 (1), 67–89.

Verma, S.; Khan, A. & Subba, U.K. (2012). Development of Psychology in India: A trend Analysis. In History of Psychology. *International Journal of Psychology*, 47 (1), 459–466.

Walsh, R.N. & Vaughan, F. (2001). Kişi Nedir? [What is Person?]. In *Ego Ötesi* [Beyond Ego] (Eds. R.N. Walsh & F. Vaughan) (Trans. H. Ekşi). İstanbul: İnsan.

Watson, J.B. (1913). Psychology as the Behaviorist Views It. *Psychological Review*, 20 (2), 158.

Watson, J.B. (1963). *Behaviorism*. Chicago: The University of Chicago Press.

Weiten, W. (2001). *Psychology Themes & Variations*. Stamford: Wadsworth.

WHO (1998). Review of The Constitution of the World Health Organization: Report of the Executive Board Special Group, 101st Session.

WHO (2021). *World Health Statistics 2021*, https://www.who.int/data/gho/publications /world-health-statistics, 19.11.2021.

Wilber, K. (1995). *Transandantal Sosyoloji* [Transcendental Sociology] (Trans. C. Polat). İstanbul: İnsan.

World Medical Association (1981). Https://Www.Wma.Net/Policies-Post/Wma-Decla ration-Of-Lisbon-On-The-Rights-Of-The-Patient/, 19.09.2019.

Wulff, D. (1997). *Psychology of Religion Classic and Contemporary*. New York: John Wiley & Sons.

Yıldırım, N. (2014). *14. Yüzyıldan Cumhuriyet'e Hastalıklar, Hastaneler, Kurumlar: Sağlık Tarihi Yazıları* [Diseases, Hospitals, Institutions from the 14th Century to the Republic: Health History Articles]. İstanbul: Tarih Vakfı Yurt Yayınları.

Yılmaz, S. (2020). Nokta-I Süveydâ'nın Önemi ve Özellikleri [Significance and Specialities of the Black Point]. *Akademiar Dergisi*, 8, 103–130.

York Al-Karam, C. (2018). Islamic Psychology: Towards a 21st Century Definition and Conceptual Framework. *Journal of Islamic Ethics*, 2 (2018), 97–109.

Yüksel, A.Ş. & Karacoşkun, M.D. (2012). Tasavvuf Psikolojisi. (Psychology of Tasawwuf). In *Din Psikolojisi El Kitabı* (Ed. M.D. Karacoşkun). Ankara: Grafiker.

Zeelenberg, M. (1999). The Use of Crying Over Spilled Milk: A note on the Rationality and Functionality of Regret. *Philosophical Psychology*, 12 (3), 325–340.

Zeelenberg, M.; Beattie, J.; Pligt, J. & Vries, N. (1996). Consequences of Regret Aversion: Effects of Expected Feedback on Risky Decision Making. *Organizational Behavior and Human Decision Processes*, 65 (2), 148–158.

Zulliger, H. (1998). *Çocuk Vicdanı ve Biz* [Child Conscience and Us] (Trans. K. Şipal). İstanbul: Cem.

Printed in the United States
by Baker & Taylor Publisher Services